HURON COUNTY LIBRARY

P9-CTA-850

HURON COUNTY LIBRARY

6492 00309791 3

Date Due

		MAY 1 1 2004	
OCT 24	MAR 3		
MAY 31	OCT 23		
MAR 8	DEC 11		
JUL 11	JUN 4		
AUG 4	OCT 24		
AUG 24	MAR 6		
JUL 3	AUG 6		
JUL 8	JUN 12		
SEP 11	MAR 24		
SEP 20	AUG 11		
JUL 16			
JUL 31			
OCT 11			
OCT 20			
APR 29			
NOV 12			

DAYT

50 Trips I

BRODART, INC.   Cat. No. 23 233   Printed in U.S.A.

917   Carpenter, Donna May Gibbs, 1954-   9046
.135   Daytripper 2 : 50 trips in and around Toronto /
404   Donna Gibbs Carpenter ; photographs by Brian Oates. --
Car   Toronto : Stoddart, 1992.
            119 p. : ill.

         "A Boston Mills Press book."
         Includes bibliographical references (p. 119)
         06058329   ISBN:1550460331 (pbk.)

         1. Toronto Region (Ont.) - Guidebooks. I. Oates, Brian.
         II. Title

2468   92SEP10   06/go   1-00579572

MERTON COUNTY LIBRARY

DAYTRIPPER 2

50 Trips In and Around Toronto

Donna Gibbs Carpenter
Photographs by Brian Oates

A BOSTON MILLS PRESS BOOK

SEP 25 1992

9046

APPRECIATION

This second volume of *Daytripper* represents hard work on the part of several people. Stephen Carpenter gladly plunged into mountains of dishes and hours of child-care that would have made a lesser man weep. C. William Gibbs reviewed each trip and Olive Gibbs provided a variety of support services. Kaitlin and Griffin are still keen daytrippers, always willing to drop their play to help mom with her book. Many thanks to all.

Canadian Cataloguing in Publication Data

Carpenter, Donna May Gibbs, 1954-
    Daytripper 2: 50 trips in and around Toronto

ISBN 1-55046-033-1

1. Toronto Region (Ont.) – Guidebooks. I. Title.

FC3097.18.C34 1992   917.13'54044   C92-093918-X
F1059.5.T683C35 1992

©Donna Gibbs Carpenter, 1992

First published in 1992 by
Stoddart Publishing Co. Limited
34 Lesmill Road
Toronto, Canada
M3B 2T6

A BOSTON MILLS PRESS BOOK
The Boston Mills Press
132 Main Street
Erin, Ontario
N0B 1T0

Winners of the
Heritage Canada
Communications Award

American Association
for State and Local History
Award Winner

Design by Gillian Stead
Edited by Noel Hudson
Typography by Justified Type Inc., Guelph
Printed in Canada by Friesen Printers

The publisher gratefully acknowledges the support of The Canada Council, Ontario Arts Council and Ontario Publishing Centre in the development of writing and publishing in Canada.

TABLE OF CONTENTS

Early York County log cabin, on the Sharon Temple grounds —photo by Donna Carpenter

PREFACE

We are so fortunate to live in Ontario. Adventures of every description lie around each bend in the road. *Daytripper* will open your eyes to places worth discovering, even though they may have existed right under your nose for years.

What is a daytrip? It's an outing lasting anywhere from a few hours to a full day. This means that you can have an interesting and invigorating holiday *and* sleep in your own bed. This also means that the trips described in *Daytripper* are within a convenient distance of home, work, family and friends. Although the trips in this book are designed to be a day's length, this doesn't mean that you can't string several of them together for a full holiday.

This volume of *Daytripper* covers the area stretching along Lake Ontario from Oakville

to Oshawa and northwards in a semi-circle encompassing Halton, Peel, York and Durham regions and southern Simcoe County. This is a diverse region, a place where city sights and country sounds are never far apart. In bustling Toronto, take in the visual richness of restored vaudeville theatres, a shop selling Chinese herbs or a historic university campus. Or leave the city behind and listen to the snap of canvas in a shipbuilding port, the creak of a millwheel, or the symphony of wind in the pines. Most of all, appreciate the way Ontario is full of surprises, supplying the traveller with haute cuisine many kilometres from the city and dramatic cliffs a stone's throw from downtown.

The number of trips possible within south-central Ontario is almost unlimited, but the following 50 have been carefully chosen. *Daytripper* has done the work of selecting the best natural and cultural features this dynamic region has to offer, and these have been presented as single-theme excursions. While each trip has a theme, it also includes several activities, so that each day is filled with variety. For example, a day spent exploring a harbour town might include a visit to a museum, a fish dinner and a historic walking tour. Each trip description includes recommendations for restaurants and picnicking spots.

Daytripper is suitable for families of all ages, single travellers and senior citizens. While many trips include a good walk or other exercise, this is not a book of rugged activities, and any of the trips can be tailored to the needs of a senior or toddler. These trips have been child-tested; well-behaved children are welcome at all the sites mentioned.

Daytripper is not just for locals. It is also aimed at tourists looking for Ontario beyond its major attractions; it can be invaluable for showing off the province to visiting relatives and friends. Take it with you on business trips, for things to do off-hours or on a rainy day.

There are a few things that daytrippers will generally not find in this book. Large, well-known attractions, such as amusement parks, will not be described. They are expensive and incompatible with the local culture and landscape. Most special events and festivals will not be described in *Daytripper*. The trips in this book are suitable over an extended season, not limited to only a week or two in the year. Any (pre-arranged) factory tours or other special-admission tours included in this book are truly visitor-friendly, since *Daytripper* adventures are meant to be spontaneous, without a great deal of advance planning.

HOW TO USE THIS BOOK

Keep it handy! You never know when you'll have a day free for an unplanned trip, so be prepared with *Daytripper* by the front door or in the glove compartment.

Make sure that you have an up-to-date, good-quality road map. For days spent outside of Metropolitan Toronto, the standard Government of Ontario highway map is very good, and the directions described in *Daytripper* assume that you have a map of at least this detail. For meandering sideroad trips when greater

map detail would be helpful, this has been noted in the trip description. A City of Toronto map indicating all streets is essential for getting around the city; it is really helpful if the map also indicates TTC (Toronto Transit Commission) routes.

Use the trip-finder on the following pages to find trips within a close drive of home, or to find trips relating to your particular hobby or interest.

The season and hours of operation for museums and other attractions sometimes change, so if a trip includes a site of special interest to you, avoid disappointment by phoning ahead to check hours of operation. This is particularly good advice for holiday periods. Phone numbers have been provided for those restaurants where reservations are recommended or where a certain restaurent is a key element in a trip. Please also phone ahead to check on wheelchair accessibility and other special needs.

It is a commonly held but erroneous belief that Toronto is an expensive city for travellers. The wise daytripper knows how to avoid parking costs by travelling TTC or by combining TTC with a low-charge or no-charge parking place. Most museums and other attractions charge an admission fee. In most cases this is a modest charge, considering the quality of the sites. You won't be disappointed. Some attractions, such as boat cruises and well-advertised amusement parks, may cost a little more than a museum, but then they offer a longer outing. The restaurants and inns suggested for daytrippers are average or inexpensive in price, unless otherwise noted. Some of the more costly places may be within limited budgets at lunchtime. Many of the trips described in this book include suggestions for picnicking, which is not only inexpensive but also a good way to really experience an area.

Don't use *Daytripper* as the last word on adventuring. Use it as a beginning, and feel free to go off discovering on your own. Ask questions of people you meet—shop owners, waiters and waitresses, and fellow travellers. Ontarians are pleased to tell of the special places within their own area. Follow their suggestions.

More happy trails to you!
Donna Gibbs Carpenter

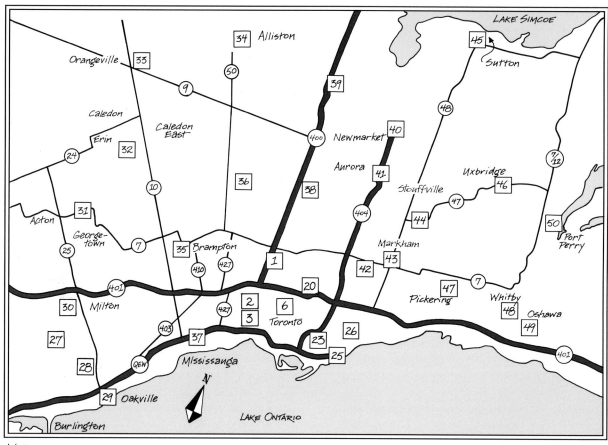

Main map

THE TRIP-FINDER

This trip-finder is an index to all 50 daytrips. Look up a topic of special interest and find the daytrip numbers listed. These numbers correspond to the number in large print at the beginning of each trip description.

ACTIVITY TRIPS

HIKING/WALKING
1,2,3,6,10,11,13,21,25,26,27,28,29,32,33,34,
35,36,37,38,39,40,41,45,47

FISHING
2,3,11,13,28,29,32,34,37,39,40,41,45,50

BIKING
2,3,11,13,25,26,27,28,32,33,34,36,38,39,
45,46,47

WINTER SPORTS
1,2,3,11,16,26,27,28,30,32,33,34,36,37,38,
43,45,47

PLEASURE DRIVING
27,32,33,38,39,45,46,47,50

SHOPPING
7,8,9,11,19,21,22,24,31,32,36,42,43,44,45,50

BOATING, CRUISES, BOAT-WATCHING
11,13,25,29,34,37,45,50

SWIMMING
13,25,28,32,34,45,50

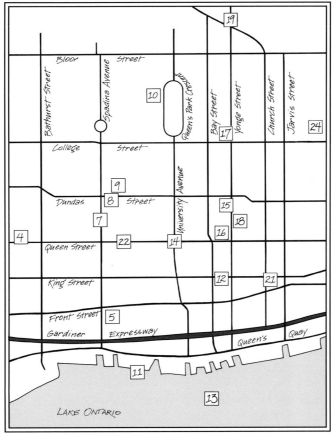

Central Toronto

THEME TRIPS

HISTORY
1,2,3,4,5,6,8,10,12,14,16,17,18,20,21,23,24,
25,26,27,28,29,30,31,32,34,35,36,37,38,40,42,
43,45,46,47,49,50

NATURE
1,2,3,13,25,26,27,28,32,33,34,36,37,38,39,
41,45,47

GARDENS
1,2,3,6,26,31,38,40,41,48,49

THEATRE/MUSIC
3,11,18,20,23,40,43,45,48

INDUSTRY/ENGINEERING
1,5,11,25,29,30,49

CULTURAL HERITAGE
9,24,27

FARMING/FARM MARKETS
2,21,23,28,30,39,44,50

VISUAL ARTS/CRAFTS
3,7,11,12,15,18,20,22,23,26,32,36,38,42,43,50

HISTORIC INNS
1,2,26,32,33,36,37,42,45,46

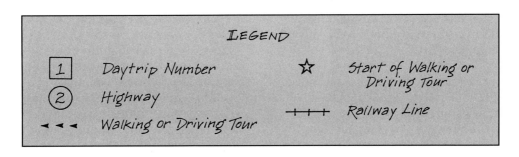

1

ETOBICOKE/NORTH YORK
Northwest Passage

Adventure happens when we are brave enough to launch ourselves into undiscovered places or points of view. The northwest corner of Metro Toronto (usually thought of as predictable and boring) has two sites that encourage daytrippers to take personal passages of two very different types. Black Creek Pioneer Village is a window into the world of wooden sidewalks, hearth fires and candlelight. The Humber Arboretum allows us to explore urban woodlands, backyard ecology and demonstration gardens.

The Humber Arboretum is on the campus of Humber College. Drive north on Highway 27 and west on Humber College Boulevard; take the first left and follow signs to the aboretum nature centre. The centre contains displays on local habitat and conservation activities, with all information geared towards the young. There may be a display on wetlands which includes tanks of critters and charts explaining the life cycle of frogs or the food chain in a pond. The emphasis is always on action— how to build a bird hotel, use shower caps as food storage covers or clean up the neighbourhood woodlot.

While the centre is open weekdays only, the 120 hectares of woods, meadow and wetland are open daily for hiking or cross-country skiing. The arboretum is known for two main "events": winter bird-watching and spring flowers. During late February bird-watchers visit the arboretum to see five species of owl, plus an abundance of wood-peckers, nuthatches and chickadees. The latter are tame enough to feed from your hand. For the botanist, spring is a rewarding time to visit the arboretum trails, for the wildflowers are abundant. There are trillium, May apple, and yellow violet, to name a few.

For those more interested in nature on the home front, the Humber campus includes demonstration gardens where you can study various styles of fencing, paving and landscaping before choosing materials and plants for the backyard. If you are inclined to leap into herb gardening, rock gardening or Oriental gardening, gather some ideas here first. The gardens are near the intersection of Humber College Boulevard and Highway 27.

Head for the next adventure in northwest Toronto. Drive north on Highway 27 and east on Steeles Avenue. Black Creek Pioneer Village is just east of Jane Street. The new visitor centre (very cleverly hidden under-ground to avoid interrupting the village scene) acts like Alice's looking glass, allowing us modern folk to pass through time to the Ontario of over a century ago. What makes Black Creek Pioneer Village unique is its comprehensiveness—over 40 buildings comprise a truly complete village. The large number of costumed guides add to the experience, with at least one guide in every building.

The Daniel Stong complex is a big draw for visitors, and since these buildings are on their original sites (all other buildings have been relocated here), they may be considered the beginnings of the village. The tiny "first" home of logs is fragrant with wood smoke and drying herbs; the two-storey "second" home (logs covered with clapboard) has the added luxury of a bake oven and a brick fireplace. Stong's farm includes a huge threshing barn (complete with Conestoga wagon, since the Stongs were Pennsylvania German), a piggery and smokehouse.

The creaking of wooden wheels and the splash of water are constant companions for visitors to Roblin's Mill, the picturesque stone building near Stong's farm. The view from the top storey, overlooking the millpond and village, is well worth the climb, and the flavour of the stone-ground flour (available for purchase) makes for rewarding baking. Near the mill are two other mainstays of early Ontario towns: a schoolhouse and church. The Fisherville Church is a simple building with box pews and wooden pulpit typical of Presbyterian churches throughout rural Ontario.

Black Creek Pioneer Village

(A very romantic spot available for weddings.) Dickson's Hill School is also typical of early Ontario, with its rows of desks and its wood stove.

Mill Road and Maple Avenue are lined with businesses: cooperage (barrel-maker), blacksmith, boot and shoe shop, cabinetmaker, printing shop, weaver, gunsmith, broom-maker, tinsmith and harness-maker. Each business allows an opportunity to see products made using old-time materials and methods. Many of these quaint shops are still in operation, selling visitors everything from tin cookie-cutters to copies of the proclamation putting a price on the head of William Lyon Mackenzie. Black Creek Pioneer Village includes the fine Burwick home (the resident upper crust) and the village doctor's home. The latter has an intriguing collection of early medical equipment: dental turnkeys and bleeding cups to make us squirm.

"Downtown" Black Creek is centred around Half Way House and Laskay's Emporium. Half Way House is a hotel and tavern, and a good stop for daytrippers who want to have a meal of stew, farmer's sausage or homemade soup. Afternoon tea is also served. (Other eateries include the Victoria Room and the Black Creek Café at the visitors centre.) Horse-drawn wagons pick up visitors outside the inn, just as they would have decades ago. Laskay's is another favourite for visitors. It is filled to the rafters with a jumble of shoehorns, fabric, dolls, fudge (exquisite!), crockery and patent medicines.

Discover a village forgotten by time. Hike an urban wilderness. Be adventurous and try a northwest passage soon.

Humber College Arboretum
Nature Centre
Monday-Friday 9:30-2:30
Grounds
Daily 8:30-dusk
(416) 675-5009

Black Creek Pioneer Village
Daily, hours vary seasonally
(416) 736-1733 (Monday-Friday)
(416) 661-6610 (taped message)

2

YORK/ETOBICOKE
Down in the Valley

Ever had the urge to follow in the footsteps of Ontario's early travellers and explorers? It's not hard to do, for the trails following the Humber River Valley in Toronto's west end have been used for thousands of years, beginning with Indians and French fur traders, and then British settlers. The ancient Humber trails now await discovery by the intrepid daytripper of the 1990s.

Start a Humber River day by picking up a picnic lunch, along with some local colour, at the Weston Farmers' Market. This market is one of the oldest in Ontario and from June to November it convenes from 8 AM to 2 PM on Saturdays. (John Street runs east of Weston Road, one block north of Lawrence Avenue.) Weston's is a small market, but this can be advantageous for those wishing to sample a diversity of wares without spending all day. The farm offerings are undeniable proof that good things do grow in Ontario: luscious berries, fresh cider, prize-winning honey, trout, homemade kielbasa and pickles. The baked goods offered by Barbara and Wendy's Country Bakery include protein-sprouted bread, cheesy cheese bread and an assortment of muffins.

Put on the pith helmet, for we're off to the wilds of the Humber Valley. Head south on Weston Road, west on Lawrence and south again on Scarlett Road. Just south of Eglinton Avenue turn west on Edenbridge Drive and continue until you reach James Gardens. (Parking, picnic sites and washrooms are located throughout the parkland.) James Gardens has a formal character, with terraced beds of ornamental shrubs, ferns and flowers. Ornamental bridges, bubbling brooks and good views over the valley make this a popular spot for wedding photos.

Walk south to Lambton Woods (the paths are signposted), one of the city's finest natural areas, very popular with bird-watchers and botanists. The trails are paved through the flat parkland (watch out for stealthy and speedy bikers) but natural through the woodlands. Upland slopes support dry forests of maple and oak, while the valley lowlands are habitat for moisture-loving plants such as jewelweed, ostrich fern, and southern Ontario's harbinger of spring, the skunk cabbage. The spring wildflower display in the upland woods is so fine that Lambton Woods has been declared a wildflower sanctuary, one of the first in North America. Search along the trail for trillium, spring beauty, hepatica and bloodroot. Don't be disappointed if you miss a spring tour, for the fall brings aster, goldenrod and witch hazel. If you are really keen for a naturalist's view of the Humber Valley, travel with a copy of Gregory and Mackenzie's *Toronto's Backyard*. It contains hints on locating and identifying such Lambton Woods flora as thimbleberry, blue beech, coltsfoot and New Jersey tea.

You can follow the Humber Valley as far south as you like. It is about 4 1/2 kilometres from James Gardens to the Old Mill near Bloor. You may choose to return to your car at James Gardens and drive west on Edenbridge and south on Royal York Road to Dundas, then take Dundas east to the entrance of tienne Brûlé Park (the entrance is just at the top of the valley slope; if you cross the river, you've gone too far). This is a pleasant tour of the river, suitable for walking, driving or picnicking. You end up at the Old Mill on Bloor Street. This magnificent stone home was built in 1848 on the site of an earlier mill, the Humber Valley being the centre of an active lumber industry. Today it is a lovely restaurant and tearoom (open daily, reservations suggested).

Both Bloor and Dundas were common routes during Ontario's early days, and numerous inns sprang up to furnish travellers with simple accommodation. One such inn remains, and it provides a fascinating look at a time when travel was not so carefree as it is today. Drive west on Bloor to Montgomery Road and follow signs to Montgomery's Inn (if

Montgomery's Inn

you miss the turn, go north on Islington to find the inn). This gracious Georgian stone residence was constructed by Thomas Montgomery about 1830; it is restored to the 1847-1850 period.

Costumed guides give congenial and informative tours of the inn. The guest room contains four lumpy double beds. A traveller would pay for one-half of a bed; another traveller could well rent the other half and crawl in beside him. This was not the imposition we might imagine: a bed mate in this large unheated room might have been welcome for extra warmth alone. The most interesting room in the inn is the pub. This is one institution that has not changed much in a century and a half. Travellers could buy cold snacks here as well as rent games (the forerunners of tabletop video games?). It is also interesting to note that the nineteenth-century version of the salted peanut was the salted cracker. They have the common purpose of encouraging guests to quench their thirst at the bar. Modern-day hospitality extends to the afternoon tea served daily in the inn basement.

In one short day we can follow the footsteps of Iroquois war parties, and of Brûlé and Brébeuf, and also frequent a nineteenth-century inn. These are just a few of the adventures awaiting you along the deeply historic and beautiful Humber Valley.

The Old Mill
(416) 236-2641

Montgomery's Inn
Monday-Friday 9:30-4:30
Saturday, Sunday & Holidays 1:00-5:00
(416) 394-8113

WEST TORONTO
High Lights

In 1890 John Howard, architect and city engineer, bequeathed his country estate, some 75 hectares including his retirement home, to the City of Toronto for use as public open space. Howard's hope was to contain the westward expansion of the city, which was threatening to overtake the countryside. Howard's plan failed to rein in the urban growth of the late 1800s, and yet it was a huge success in providing the city with the embryo of its largest green space, beloved High Park.

High Park now totals about 160 hectares and is accessible by auto or TTC (take the subway to High Park or the bus south on Keele). Start a High Park day seeing it through nineteenth-century eyes—visit delightful Colborne Lodge,

located on Howard Avenue near the south end of the park.

Colborne (built in 1837) is unique among Toronto's historical sites because it is a modest Regency-style cottage, first and foremost a woodsy retreat and not a grand house. Regency homes were designed to be romantic imitations of cottages in Imperial India, and Colborne illustrates the trademarks of the style, with a wide canopied veranda, low-pitched hip roof and multi-paned French doors. Colborne Lodge was situated, with artistic effect, high on a hill overlooking oak woodlands, with plans for views of the lodge and its surroundings.

After a knock on the side door of the house, costumed guides usher you in and provide an

Colborne Lodge

informative tour of the home. Most of the furnishings are original, as are the hundreds of paintings done by Howard himself (art master at Upper Canada College). This extensive collection makes Colborne the best place in the city to get a good idea of what old York was like, with paintings of the town from every possible vantage point.

Just because Colborne has an informal ambience doesn't mean that it was without comfort. Just the opposite: since Howard was a civil engineer, his cottage had indoor plumbing (some say the first in the city). What does the famous room look like? At first glance, very much like the bathroom of today, until the guide points out that the toilet probably drained to a nearby hillside, that the bathtub lacked a drain and had to be emptied by bucket, and that the hot water came from a tank in the room above, filled by hand (a doubtful improvement for servants). Because common opinion held that indoor plumbing was unhygienic (Toronto had its share of cholera and typhoid), the door to the lavatory was hidden by the wallpaper pattern so as not to embarass or alarm guests, who would still travel to the loo in the backyard.

Whether the activity takes places in the summer kitchen, the basement winter kitchen or on the lawns outside, there's usually something interesting going on at Colborne, especially during kids' summer programs and the Dickens Christmas festivities. But enough for Colborne Lodge, it is time to step outside and see the result of Howard's generosity.

Grenadier Pond, just downhill from Colborne Lodge, is High Park's most famous feature. In summer it is used for fishing and model-boat sailing. During the winter most of the pond freezes, providing a natural skating rink. The small marsh area at the north end of the pond does not freeze, making it a good place for naturalists to find wintering waterfowl. During the spring, birders head for the bushier areas on the west side of the pond to see migrating songbirds.

High Park is prime picnic territory, with countless spots, ranging from high-profile sites among manicured flower gardens to romantic hide-a-ways in more natural woodsy areas. If it's the cook's day off, enjoy a meal at the Grenadier Restaurant, a well-kept budget secret. The menu is Toronto international, with

souvlaki, meatloaf, roast pork, and moussaka; six courses of home cooking for under $5 (open daily year-round).

There are hectares of rock gardens, rose gardens and a water garden for walking off the lunch. High Park is one of the few places in Toronto where you can wander through an oak forest that looks more like jolly old England than southern Ontario. Bikers adore the challenge of High Park's hilly roadways, and best of all, cars are banned on Sundays from May to October. Tots enjoy the playgrounds, duck ponds, sports fields, wading pool and small zoo, home to yaks, bison, deer and peacocks. During the winter there are cross-country ski trails, weather permitting.

A High Park day lasts well past dark, since you can enjoy Shakespeare under starry skies during the summer run of *The Dream in High Park* by the Toronto Free Theatre (performed near the Grenadier Restaurant in the middle of the park). The plays are free, although a modest contribution is suggested. In addition, there are Sunday-afternoon concerts during the summer months.

In High Park, the city has a generous green space for play, wildlife, gardens, fishing, theatre, hiking and biking. And, like the original endowment, it is all entirely free. John Howard, bless his generous soul, must be pleased.

Colborne Lodge
Monday-Saturday 9:30-5:00
Sundays & Holidays 12:00-5:00
(416) 595-1567

Toronto Free Theatre
(The Dream in High Park)
Tuesday-Saturday evenings
Saturday matineé
(416) 368-2856

DOWNTOWN
Dig into the Past

"Dig into the past." That's the catch phrase for a unique Toronto Board of Education program in which members of the community act as volunteer archaeologists, unearthing buildings and artifacts of early Toronto. It may sound odd, but scratching in the dirt at the Trinity-Bellwoods dig site is a captivating experience. A few hours as an amateur archaeologist can be combined with a visit to historic Fort York for a day spent digging into Toronto's past.

Trinity-Bellwoods Park runs between Queen and Dundas streets a few blocks west of Bathurst Street and is easily accessible by TTC. Phone the Archaeological Resource Centre a few days ahead of your visit to make reservations. (Plan on spending at least half a day.)

Don't expect to dig in to your work right away. Field staff take time to describe the checkered history of the site. The dig is concerned with a rural estate, "Gore Vale," built in 1820 by Duncan Cameron, Provincial Secretary of Upper Canada. During the twentieth century Gore Vale was part of Trinity College and then a boys' club. In a strange variation of modern urban development, the house was demolished to make way for parkland. The archaeological dig has unearthered building segments and artifacts from Cameron's rural retreat as well as from the 1940s victory housing which once stood here. Some of the thousands of artifacts unearthed to date are on display in the site trailer.

Professional staff do an excellent job of preparing and equipping volunteers, and explaining the use of trowel, bucket, screen, grid paper and coding system for "finds." And then you set to it, carefully scraping a thin layer of soil away from one of the 2-metre-square pits, describing and mapping anything found, sifting soil and then discarding it. (The pits may be a few centimetres to a few metres deep; one contains a considerable amount of wall, chimney, and roofing

materials, others materials from the victory housing.) The digging process is brightened by the surroundings: a peaceful green park and the congenial company of staff and volunteers (and there can be lots of people here, from school classes to neighbourhood seniors). How rewarding to uncover a bit of old crockery or a square century-old nail and to speculate on how and when it was last used.

There's nothing like a few hours of fresh air and exercise to perk up an appetite. A few blocks east of the dig site on Queen Street is Future Bakery, the building with the lively murals of bakers at work. Future's bread, featuring rye in several variations, is so revered that customers line up at dawn to buy straight from the loading docks. Check out the display cases for breads festooned with braids, flowers and foliage, all in dough. The cafeteria has stick-to-your-ribs cooking like cabbage rolls, varenykys and borscht. The dessert case offers rum balls, raspberry bombe and white chocolate-hazelnut cake—not for the calorie-phobe. (Bakery and café open daily.)

Now, back from the Future and on to Historic Fort York. The grand-daddy of Toronto historic sites is located off Fleet Street, just west of Bathurst; it's accessible by car or Bathurst streetcar. Start your visit in the barracks house, where museum displays tell the interesting story of the fort. Toronto's European settlement began when a palisaded garrison was constructed on this very site in 1793; the fort quickly became the centre of social and economic life in the town. In 1812 Fort York was attacked by a large American force; the fort was surrendered and the town looted. Between 1813 and 1816 Fort York was rebuilt and its defences strengthened. The fort's eight buildings date to this period of reconstruction.

Costumed guides offer a tour of the cramped, hot, smelly barracks which were provided for common soldiers and their families. Imagine rough cast walls, one common pot of stew,

Historic Fort York

constant drill and the threat of flogging. Contrast this life with that illustrated in the officers' barracks: whitewashed walls, private rooms, personal servants, and meals comprising a dozen dishes. The blockhouse is now a small theatre which plays a multi-screen slide show on the War of 1812. Don't miss this excellent presentation which handily capsulizes historical events and, more importantly, highlights the influence of the war on Canadian identity and Canadian-American relations. The Fort York staff work hard at establishing an authentic atmosphere, with demonstrations of musketry, drills, music and cooking.

There are some interesting connections between Fort York and Gore Vale. Many of the married officers at the garrison would have had homes along Queen Street in the vicinity of Gore Vale. Since Fort York and Gore Vale are contemporaries, similar types of domestic items have been found at each site. Fort York is a successful living museum

because of the efforts of archaeologists in unearthing buildings, domestic implements and military gear.

Digging into history is a lot more fun than it was during school days of old. Not only do we get to fulfill childhood dreams of discovering buried treasure, but we get to see how our efforts might eventually be used to re-create Canadian history.

Archaeological Resource Centre
(Toronto Board of Education)
Volunteer hours:
May-October: Monday-Friday 9:00-3:00
Also June-September: Saturday 9:00-4:00
(416) 393-0665

Historic Fort York
Daily 9:30-5:00
(416) 392-6907

DOWNTOWN
Be a Good Sport

Let's play ball! He shoots, he scores! Touchdown! Toronto reverberates with the sounds of professional sport. It seems like the glitz of the major leagues is an integral part of big-city life. While watching a game can make for a good day, just as interesting a time can be had by visiting some of Toronto's shrines to sport.

Begin the day on the Canadian National Exhibition grounds, at the building which houses the Hockey Hall of Fame and Museum and the Canada Sports Hall of Fame. (The Hockey Hall of Fame will be revamped and relocated to Yonge and Front streets in 1992.) The Sports Hall of Fame looks at our national character through our heroes and their achievements in several sports. Displays of text, photos and equipment introduce us to the likes of Sylvia Burka, "Jackrabbit" Johannsen, Terry Fox and Johnny Longden.

The Hockey Hall of Fame is the place to find hockey's greatest memorabilia—more sweaters, masks, skates and glittering trophies than you thought existed. The exhibits are organized chronologically: first formations (1880-1925), the NHL emerges (1927-1945), the dynasty years (1946-1966), and expansion and the international arena (1967 onward). The photos and bios of yesteryear's personalities are all here. Sit in a comfortable theatre for replays of thrilling moments in Canada's favourite sport.

Drive along Front Street towards the Skydome. If it's time for lunch, head north on Portland to its intersection with King. The Rotterdam restaurant and brew pub is popular with sports fans. The Rotterdam serves over 200 varieties of beer, as well as inexpensive lunchtime specials.

Drive to the Skydome and head for the souvenir-and-gift shop (by gate 4) for tour tickets. (Call a day ahead to check on times, as tours vary according to the Dome schedule.) While visitors wait for the guide, they can study detailed exhibits on the history of the Dome site and its development from navy wharf to major entertainment facility. The displays include a fascinating collection of nineteenth-century objects found during excavation.

The tour begins with *The Inside Story*, a multi-image film on Dome construction. Architect Roderick Robbie and structural engineer Michael Allen are shown wrestling with a design challenge, the completely retractable roof that makes this building unlike anything previously attempted. Facts come at you thick and fast: the Dome represents 12,000 man-years of labour; 32-storeys tall, it contains more concrete than two CN Towers; the roof is designed to cope with 3 1/2-metre snowdrifts and can open in 20 minutes. Steelworkers describe working in weather so cold that they couldn't feel the nuts and bolts they held in their hands. (American visitors love that one.) The camera work has you sitting on workers' shoulders as they grip a girder with their legs and lean into space to guide large roof members into place. Talk about being rivetted to your seat.

The tour takes you to several vantage points within Skydome. Sit in padded Sky Club seats in the press box and peek into a coveted Skybox—and then hear the price of each of these seats (even more than you paid for parking). The tour goes through the Toronto Argos dressing room, but not the $2-million Jays enclave. Enter the playing field from the visitors' dugout and see the field from a player's-eye view (you can use the players' fountain and hand basin on the way through). On the field, find out how the pitcher's mound disappears when the field is used for football.

Jay's paraphernalia of every description is sold in the Skydome gift shop. The Athletic Supply Store across Front Street sells caps, sweats, shirts and other clothes emblazoned with team logos from across North America. There's also a terrific collection of action posters from baseball, hockey and basketball.

Fans at Skydome

Head by TTC or car to Maple Leaf Gardens on Carlton near Yonge. (Streetcar to University and then subway to College/Carlton; or drive along Front to Church and north to Carlton.) The Gardens has been called one of Canada's two most important religious buildings, the other being the Montreal Forum. Like the Dome, the Gardens is a construction marvel. Hundreds of workers laboured around the clock to complete the building in time for the 1931 hockey season. The project was finished in a miraculous five months. At the time of construction the Gardens was an architectural oddity because it lacked interior pillars. This gives each patron a perfect view of the ice surface.

Entering the Gardens is very much like a trip down memory lane, with the foyer decorated with black-and-white photos of Maple Leafs—Conacher, Clancy, Baun, Horton . . . the list seems endless. There's no lavish decoration here; the scent of blood, sweat and tears seems to hang in the air. The Gardens auditorium is not open on a regular schedule. In the southeast corner of the Gardens, Leafsports sells team sweaters from across the NHL.

Whether you play in the major leagues or in the sand lot, you'll enjoy a day filled with Toronto's sports history, heroes and stadia.

Canada's Sports Hall of Fame
Daily 10:30-4:30
(extended hours during CNE)
(416) 595-1046

Hockey Hall of Fame and Museum
Mid-September to mid-May:
Daily 10:00-4:30
Mid-May to September:
Monday-Friday 10:00-5:00
Saturday & Sunday 10:00-7:00
(extended hours during CNE)
(416) 595-1345

Skydome Tours
Daily 10:00-4:00
Availability varies with Dome schedule
(416) 341-2770

MIDTOWN
Everyone's Home is Their Casa

For about a century and a half, Torontonians have displayed their success in commerce and public affairs by building august mansions. The difficulty has always been to balance a need for privacy with a desire to make a public statement in housing. Mother Nature helped solve the dilemma for some Torontonians by providing an escarpment, the shoreline of glacial Lake Iroquois: homes built on the hill are separated from the city and yet highly visible. Spend a day on a home-and-garden tour along the escarpment and see one of Toronto's loveliest neighbourhoods.

Begin at Spadina House at 285 Castle Road (just east of Casa Loma). The estate first belonged to the Baldwin family, who built a country cottage here early in the last century. It was the Baldwins who gave us wide Spadina Avenue, carved out of the forest so that the family could have a view of Lake Ontario. The mansion which commands that view today was built by the Austin family in 1866 and renovated around the turn of the century.

If you can tour just one historic property in the city, make it Spadina. Unlike most historic homes which are furnished "to period," Spadina's furnishings are original to the house, nothing having been added or removed from generations of family life. Tours of the house begin with a 15-minute film on the history of this 50-room mansion with the remarkable glass-and-iron carriage porch. Tour guides draw attention to a myriad of details, such as radiator covers carved with squirrels and owls (representing industry and wisdom) and settees designed for ladies wearing bustles. A tour of Spadina becomes a rare peek into Victorian life as you learn about sleeping in an upright position and how to make thumb-print cookies. The story continues outside, where the Toronto Garden Club has restored the grounds to their former beauty with over 300 kinds of plants, many of them rare varieties popular during the Victorian era.

The basement of Spadina is filled with displays on historic restoration. Read stories about scraps of wallpaper and paint samples being chemically analyzed so that they could be faithfully reproduced, and about hidden fireplaces discovered during restoration.

Say a fond goodbye to Spadina and hello to the daydream in stone next door, Casa Loma. Sir Henry Pellatt's wealth came from his railways and electric light companies (he built the Canadian Electric generating plant at Niagara). A nut for castles, he copied bits and pieces of his European favourites and had Edward Lennox (architect of Old City Hall and the Provincial Legislature) pull it all together. Even the desk in his study is a copy, the original belonging to Napoleon. Alas, the cost of construction, upkeep (no less than 40 servants to run a castle) and business ruin cost Sir Henry his fortune and he was forced to sell his home and its furnishings.

This is a great place for kids. They can climb the towers, grimace at gargoyles, explore the 300-metre underground tunnel to the stables and discover a secret passageway. Adults marvel at the craftmanship. For example, Peacock Alley, a hallway copied from Windsor Castle, has a 6-centimetre-thick floor held together not with nails, but with mahogany-and-rosewood joiners. The white marble bathroom has a shower with six heads and a phone by the tub. The stables—works of art in mahogany and marble—are more comfortable than many homes.

There are a number of streets in the Casa Loma area that should be explored on this trip. Topography and urban design have conspired against easy travel, with many dead ends and one-way streets. Spare your car and your nerves by finding an area that appeals, and then touring by foot.

Head north on Bathurst to Alcina and turn west. Alcina and neighbouring streets present a fascinating mix of architectural styles, as

Casa Loma

most older homes have been restored or renovated. The result is modern stucco beside rustic log cabin beside original brick. At Wychwood, head south for a peek at a unique residential area and a national historic area, Wychwood Park. This is private property, so you must be satisfied with the view from the gate. Head west along Tyrrell and south down Christie to Hillcrest Park. This park has a sweeping view over the city and is rarely crowded. A good place to picnic today.

East of Casa Loma is the southern part of Forest Hill, perhaps the last bastion of dignified living in Toronto. Find Poplar Plains Road, Russell Hill Road or Warren Road and follow one of them north of St. Clair, where the houses are even larger and more handsome. This is very agreeable walking or biking territory. Picnic spots may be found at the Churchill Reservoir at St. Clair and Spadina.

Home-and-garden tours are a popular pastime, offering the chance to see a privileged way of life as well as the best in residential architecture. A daytrip along Toronto's escarpment is a home-and-garden tour that can't be beat.

Spadina House
Monday-Saturday 9:30-4:15
Sundays & Holidays 12:00-4:15
(416) 392-6910

Casa Loma
Daily 10:00-4:00
(416) 923-1171

DOWNTOWN
A Stitch in Time

Fashion is one of those curious junctions where fine art and street culture meet. Toronto is a great place for exploring the world of fashion and fabric, whether you are using the vantagepoint of designer, artisan, shopper or home seamstress. Much more than just a shopping spree, a daytrip to Toronto's fashion district can include a textile museum tour and a visit to a delicious remnant of the original Jewish needle-trade area.

The Museum for Textiles is located at 45 Centre Street, behind the new City Hall. It ranges over four floors, with spacious galleries, an area for juried shows of contemporary fabric artists, and a research area for professionals working in theatre and film. The museum also includes an interesting gift shop that carrys fabric artifacts from around the world, as well as books on clothing design and textiles.

The Museum for Textiles is a celebration of beauty in fabric, whether in hooked rugs from Nova Scotia, embroidered blouses from Bolivia or beaded baby carriers from Borneo. Although textiles from around the globe are displayed, the most enchanting come from Asia, particularly Indonesia, the country with the richest variety of textiles in the world. There is delicate embroidery using gold-wrapped thread and miniature mirrors, and silk batiks in a collage of colours.

The exhibits are always changing, but usually include information on some aspect of fabric manufacture. For example, we can follow the

Museum for Textiles

story of fabric dyeing from prehistory through medieval English craft guilds to the present age of computer-controlled manufacture. Or learn how, in Africa, fabric design is used to record important family and community events, and how brocade religious vestments developed their particular form.

It is time to explore Toronto's textile and garment district. Catch the Dundas streetcar just north of the museum and head west to Spadina Avenue, the heart of Toronto's fashion district. Spadina, from Front to College, is lined with shops, small and large, selling clothing (from high falutin' to homespun), furs and leather goods, millinery, fabrics, jewellery—pretty much everything possible for personal adornment.

Here are a few Spadina landmarks and unusual shops to whet your appetite. They are listed generally north to south.

Trans European Textile Dry Goods (370) is a happy melange of cottons, brocades, velvets and polyesters. Evex Importers (355) has a huge stock of leather goods, such as purses, knapsacks and a profusion of luggage. Rothman's Hat Shop (345) carries men's and ladies' millinery of every kind, from Stetsons to berets. It is a tiny shop, but typical of the way Spadina looked for decades.

If it's time for a lunch break, Switzer's Deli at number 322 is the only restaurant to consider. It is a holdover from when Spadina was the centre of Toronto's Jewish community and at least a half-dozen good deli's were in the immediate vicinity. Alas, only Switzer's is left; let's hope that it does not relocate to North York, as so many others have. In the meantime, savour smoked meats in a dozen varieties, as well as knish, lox, gefilte and blintz. The prices are great and the service makes one feel right at home.

There are several shops for the pin-cushion set along Queen west of Spadina. Textile Importers (493 Queen West) has a notions department that is bigger than most stores, with an enormous selection of appliqués, wood and plastic beads, fabric paints and fake fur. Looking for a button to match one of those the dryer ate? Head for Textile Importers. World Sewing Centre (511) has a machine for every seamstress and Neverens Tailoring Supplies (451) has an excellent supply of scissors and other necessities.

The Spadina-Queen area offers two types of specialty shops. First, there are the furriers— and there are dozens of them, clustered around 150-250 Spadina. Paul Magder is notorious for his court battles over the Sunday shopping laws. There's also Cats, Peter Makos, Sellers-Gough, Royal and Cosmopolitan, to name a few; Adelaide Street is home to several others. Perfect Leather Goods (192 Spadina) has a huge inventory, from trench coats to suits in every shade.

The fashion district's second specialty is bridal goods. Don't miss Sussman's Bridal Supply at 420 Queen West: two floors of veils, hat forms, gloves and miles of imported lace. Sussman's is worth a peek even if you're just a lover of exquisitely beautiful things. There are several other bridal stores on Spadina, such as Bridal Fashions (241), Ms. Bridal (141) and Bride Beautiful (101).

Spadina south of Queen is a treasure trove of bargains. The kids' and women's clothing at Suzy's (154) are incredibly cheap—those aren't size stickers, that's the price. Also visit Simons Warehouse Outlet (129) and Sonnydale Fashions (147). Windsor Frocks (146) sells lovely things to wear "after 5," as does Concorde Import (148). If you are shopping for kids' wear, don't miss Winners (57) for popular labels at good prices.

The list of places to visit in Toronto's fashion district could go on forever, but there's only one way to find your own special store, and that is to make Spadina Avenue and the Museum for Textiles a daytrip soon. There may be no more enjoyable way to save a few dollars.

Museum for Textiles
Tuesday-Friday 11:00-5:00
Saturday & Sunday 12:00-5:00
(416) 599-5515

Many shops open Sunday

DOWNTOWN
Toronto Then and Now

One of the best places to appreciate Toronto's 150-year metamorphosis from farmland into cosmopolitan metropolis is in the Baldwin-McCaul-Beverley Street vicinity. In one day we can visit a rural estate of the early 1800s, a city home of the late 1800s, and explore a neighbourhood where the relaxed pace of the past is combined with a lively modern outlook.

Begin the tour through time at the city's favourite historic home, the Grange, located immediately behind the Art Gallery of Ontario on Dundas Street. (Ride the Dundas streetcar west from the University subway line and disembark at Beverley.) The Grange was the home of the D'Arcy Boulton family and was built around 1817; it is the oldest remaining brick home in Toronto. Painstakingly accurate restoration work and costumed interpreters paint a picture of genteel country life, for at the time of construction the Grange would have been far removed from town.

The Boulton family created a facsimile of an English estate, complete with red-brick Georgian house and extensive gardens. The front entrance hall, with a breathtakingly beautiful staircase and stained-glass window, is a fitting introduction to a home filled with Georgian and Regency furniture. Some of the furnishings were original to the Boultons and bear the family crest. The main floor of the Grange is dominated by a formal dining room set for tea. Typical of the era, it is in the basement where most of the action occurs, for this is where the large staff would have bustled about, performing the business of the household. Those activities are recreated for visitors, and the kitchen often has some tasty examples of baking typical of the early 1800s.

During the late nineteenth century the town of York grew up quickly around the Grange, and Beverley Street became a very fashionable address. Walk north on Beverley. It is not hard to imagine the street as it appeared during the 1870s, when the Second Empire style with mansard roof was all the rage. For about 120 years the most striking building on Beverley has been the Italian consulate at the corner of Beverley and Dundas.

For a look at life a generation removed from the Grange, stop at the corner of Beverley and Baldwin for a tour of George Brown House (1875). This solid-looking home was built by George Brown, one of the Fathers of Confederation, an avid political reformer and the founder of the *Globe* newspaper. (In the famous painting of the Confederation meeting in Charlottetown, Brown is seated in front, the long, lean, red-haired Scot.) Like the Grange before it, Brown's home soon became a centre for social and political life in the city.

George Brown House is largely unfurnished since it is rented out for meetings—and what a setting for your wedding or company "do." But a half-hour tour through panelled rooms combines with excellent historic photographs to provide a detailed depiction of how the home would have appeared. The front hall achieves a formal Victorian look with its ornately carved staircase and original coloured floor tiles; the hall is a copy of the entrance to the Lieutenant-Governor's residence (now demolished). The basement houses displays on the history of the house and best of all, a video presentation that makes George Brown and his home come alive.

So much for Toronto of the past. Let's explore the Toronto of the twentieth century. Just as the Grange and George Brown House served as centre of everything vital to the city in the 1800s, so the lively neighbourhood around Baldwin and McCaul serves as a place where contemporary ideas mingle and mature before becoming fashionable (thanks to the influence of the students from the nearby Ontario College of Art). This area manages to remain vigorous and yet distinctly laid-back—the last place in the city to experience a little bit of the '60s.

George Brown House

Whereas the Toronto of the Grange and George Brown House was very British, the Toronto of today is cosmopolitan. Travel the restaurants of Baldwin and sample food from around the world. French continental fans can head for highly rated La Botega and Le Petit Gaston. The Bahamian Kitchen is a relative newcomer, with conch and curry to warm your heart. At renowned Kowloon the dim sum lunch and wonderful soups are sure to please. Malaysian food (cheap, plentiful and flavourful) is offered at Sri Malaysia and Ole Malacca. Vegetarians head for Yolfi's (sandwiches and nachos) or Mandel's creamery, an authentic kosher dairy that makes delectable cream cheese. It's a great pleasure to sit in the leafy shade by the Yung Sing Bakery, surveying the street scene while munching on a pastry filled with black-bean pâté.

Baldwin is not just eating. Morningstar, clothier to the granola set, has a store here, with comfy clothes (much from Asia) at good prices. Use the savings to visit Letki silversmiths (ready-made or custom-designed pieces), Around Again Records or Baldwin Books.

Although we can't know for sure what the Boultons or the Browns would have thought of today's Baldwin Street, one might guess that they would have appreciated how this delightful community keeps their family homes at the centre of the best in Toronto.

The Grange
Tuesday-Sunday 12:00-4:00
Also Wednesday 6:00-9:00
(416) 977-0414

George Brown House
Wednesday 1:00-4:00
Sunday 12:00-4:00
(416) 324-6969

DOWNTOWN
Orient Yourself

Ride the Dundas streetcar west from the University subway line. As you approach Huron Street, you'll see a montage of signs in Chinese characters, hear a hundred voices bartering over fresh lychees, and smell the mixed aroma of raw poultry and coffee houses. Whether these sights, sounds and smells are comfortingly familiar or seductively exotic, the traveller is lured off the streetcar for a deeper exploration of Chinatown.

Begin your orientation on a Sunday, when Chinatown is at its most vivacious. Disembark the streetcar at Huron (ask the driver to call the stop); the section of Dundas from Huron to Spadina has the greatest concentration of Chinese businesses. At first look the streetscape may appear to be a confusing jumble of shops and restaurants. Chinatown is actually made up of a few basic elements (grocers, teahouses, import shops, herbalists and bakeries) that are repeated in seemingly endless variety. Visit each type of establishment to gain an appreciation for the entire neighbourhood.

First there are the grocery stores, chock-full of unusual items. Pick up all the ingredients for authentic Asian cooking—dried mushrooms, barbecued duck, wonton wrappers, lotus flowers and bok choy. The wide variety of merchandise at the Kien-Nan Trading Company (70 Huron Street) makes it ideal for browsing. Upstairs, Far East Food Products wholesales 10,000 fortune cookies daily.

Chinatown —photo by Donna Carpenter

Don't miss the import shops, as they are sure bets for gift shopping, selling embroidered silk pyjamas and table linens at bargain prices. They also carry kites, wind chimes, ornamental screens, fans and jewellery. The Chung Mee Trading Company (437 Dundas) and Hoy Kun Trading Company (436) can provide several hours of rummaging and purchasing.

Chinatown's most interesting shops belong to the herbalists. These tiny, aromatic emporiums act as windows to a different culture, offering homemade and packaged remedies for any ailment, ancient or modern. Po Sung Herbs and Health Foods at 18 Huron offers over 100 concoctions made from such items as musk, ginseng or essence of chicken. Nam Pek Hong Dong Chinese Herb Centre at 393 Dundas sells 800 varieties of herbs.

Any Chinatown would be incomplete without a good tea shop, and the Ten Ren Tea Company at the corner of Dundas and Huron is held in high esteem. Ornately carved tables are set with Chinese teacups and brewing equipment, ready for customers to leisurely sample the wares prior to purchase. The shop sells dozens of tea varieties, including jasmine, chrysanthemum and oolong, as well as fermented black teas.

One of the delights of a day in Chinatown is a visit to the bakeries. The Kim Moon Bakery at 438 Dundas and the Melewa Bakery (433), among others, appear equally crowded with customers. You'll come away with several samples of pastries filled with lotus, black bean or chestnut paste. Add to that egg tarts, almond cookies, sponge cake and huge buns filled with spiced meat or beans, and you have the makings of a gastronomic splurge.

The Chinatown strip along Dundas also includes magazine and newspaper shops, Chinese typesetters, and Chinese paralegal services. If art is your thing, head for the Karwah Gallery (289 Dundas), which sells paintings and prints (you'll quickly pick up the Chinese reverence for nature art). Chinatown even has room for one Japanese shop, the Furuya Trading Company at 460 Dundas— the only place in the area for cash-and-carry sushi.

A recent addition to the Dundas scene is the Chinese shopping mall. The Dragon City complex at Dundas and Spadina is a modern two-storey mall with furniture and clothing stores, an aquarium shop, pharmacy, and a cafeteria area with foods from across Asia.

If you went overboard at the bakeries, then you are in an understandable but regrettable dilemma, because lunch is the next stop. Chinatown offers visitors two special lunches, dim sum and Peking duck. Dim sum is a wonderful experience. Trolleys stacked with morsel-sized treats are wheeled from table to table; you just point at what you would like, from shrimp wrapped in pastry to custard tarts. Dim sum is always a hit with kids. Chinese etiquette demands that there be no leftovers, for the price is calculated on the empty steamer baskets. Peking duck is a multi-course meal of crispy duck served with sauce and a multitude of veggies.

A notable dim sum restaurant is the Hsin Kuang at 346 Spadina. You can't miss this yellow-and-green palace guarded by lions and heavy doors. This is a very popular spot for noisy family groups; sometimes it seems that every large family in the city is here. The Champion House Restaurant (478 Dundas) is reputed to have the best Peking duck in Toronto. Other often recommended restaurants are Chinatown International (421 Dundas) and Lee Gardens (358 Spadina); the latter serves terrific food at budget prices.

Chinatown is rapidly changing as recent immigrants from Vietnam appear on the scene with their own restaurants and import shops concentrated on Spadina north of Dundas. The best way to sample Vietnamese Toronto is to visit a coffee house, where coffee is served with ice and/or condensed milk.

At the end of a day of browsing, bargain-hunting and grazing your way through the better part of Torontonian Asia, hop back on the "Orient Express" —the Dundas streetcar—and head for home. Then stretch out in your silk pyjamas and luxuriate over Chinese tea, satisfied that another trip to the exotic Orient is only a TTC token away.

DOWNTOWN
Grounds for Higher Education

Smack dab in the middle of Toronto is a wonderful land of gardens, gargoyles, football games and colleges. The University of Toronto's expansive and very beautiful campus is often overlooked by daytrippers because many of us are hesitant to enter the inner sanctums of academia. Don't let this reluctance keep you from a day of great architecture, a resident ghost, carillon concerts and eating on the cheap.

"U of T" operates year-round. From September to April the campus throbs with activity. During the summer it is wonderfully serene and personable student tour guides operate from Hart House.

Travel via subway to the Museum stop (University line). Walk south on Queen's Park Crescent to Gothic Hart House. A gift from the Massey family (Massey as in Massey Hall, Massey-Ferguson, and Raymond and Vincent Massey), Hart House was built between 1911 and 1919. It is the social centre of campus, intended to round out academic life with four eateries, a library (no studying, only leisure reading), theatre, meeting and music rooms, an art gallery (Canadiana), a tuck shop, two gyms and a pool. The Great Hall is straight out of Hampton Court Palace—hammerbeam ceiling, glorious coloured windows, and panels decorated with university crests. It's also a spot for good food at great prices.

Walk past the Soldier's Tower at the west end of Hart House. The tower houses a carillon (musical bells), one of 600 in the world, and on Sundays during summer the delicate sound of bells floats over the old campus as dusk brings a lovely peace to the scene. Continue around King's College Circle, pausing to watch soccer, football or rugby on the lawn known as front campus.

The next building, University College, is acknowledged as a national architectural masterpiece, although when it was constructed in the late 1850s, critics were not impressed with its combination of classical, medieval and flamboyant Victorian styles. University College is the result of the province secularizing Anglican King's College, and it was important that the building present a non-ecclesiastical image. Diversity was "in," and it is reflected in several ways. Each entry is decorated with columns, each column carved unlike any other. The elaborate and heavy carvings inside the building—the gargoyles represent porters' views of their bosses—are also completely individual. The college gryphon on the eastern staircase has a polished finish, since students believe a touch of the gryphon will bring good luck on exams.

The Croft Chapter House, the rounded building at the southwest corner of the college, was Canada's first chemistry laboratory, the conical roof designed to accommodate noxious fumes. It is also the centre of the university's greatest legend, that of Reznikoff, the ghost of a stonemason who, while working on the college, was killed in a fight over a woman. Reznikoff was thrown into the well of the centre tower (the one with a single asymmetrical turret), and it is said that his ghost haunts the college to this day. A gargoyle on the wall of Croft Chapter House near where the house meets the college (half-hidden by ivy) is said to be a likeness of poor Reznikoff.

The university is actually a community of colleges, each having a religious affiliation (excepting University College) and most were established during the late 1800s. Students register through one college, and each college maintains residences, chapels, theology classes and social activities. A U of T tour must include a college or two, for not only are they handsome buildings, but they are the best places to observe student life.

The first of the church colleges on the tour is Presbyterian Knox College (1911), on the western edge of King's College Circle. The entrance opens onto two grand staircases, one

Student Council Building, University of Toronto (formerly the Observatory)

Knox College Courtyard, University of Toronto

Trinity College Chapel, University of Toronto

leading to the library and the other to the chapel. These spacious rooms, identical in design, feature cold grey walls countered by marvellous golden windows. Don't miss the Knox College courtyard. Stone doorways and stairs and leaded windows present a scene that is straight out of Oxford. Knox, like much of U of T, has been the backdrop for dozens of feature films, each fooling the audience into believing the setting is England.

At the south end of King's College Circle is Convocation Hall, another building that is held dear by Torontonians, although not welcomed by architects at the time of its construction (1906). It is used for concerts, special lectures, classes and, of course, convocations. Graduating students march from Hart House along King's College Circle to this round Edwardian flourish to finish their university careers.

Walk east from front campus and across Queen's Park, passing baroque St. Michael's College (Roman Catholic, 1856), a centre of medieval studies. Just north of St. Michael's is Methodist Victoria College. In a city built of Victorian architecture, it is no small thing to say that the main college building is a remarkable structure. It dates to 1892 and uses every architectural trick going—gargoyles, turrets, ornamental stonework—to give its three storeys the look of many more. In marked contrast, the interior, including the chapel, is restrained and cool.

The last college of the day is on Hoskin Avenue, so cross Queen's Park again (beware of the rapidly moving traffic). Trinity (High Anglican, 1925) is a fine example of British scholastic architecture, a combination of Gothic and Tudor elements. Peeking out of the arched windows onto the cloistered inner courtyard with its immaculate lawn, one is sure that Henry VIII is about to enter for a game of tennis. Trinity College represents the protest of Anglicans against secular education. The Trinity Chapel is a highlight of a U of T tour. The chapel was not designed until 1955, and it is remarkable how it harmonizes with the rest of the college. The windows are tall and narrow, with sparse touches of colour; the feel is airy and majestic, very reverent. An appropriate climax to a day of beautiful buildings.

Where students hang out there is bound to be cheap food. The strip along Bloor from Avenue Road to Bathurst has a number of restaurants suitable for today's trip. L'Europe, the Continental and the Old Country, holdovers from when the area was Hungarian, serve schnitzel, goulash and dumplings at yesterday's prices. The biggest flavour sensation in the vicinity is at Lisa's (286 Bloor West), where fresh fruit and spring water are mixed to create Toronto's own gelato fresco. Flavours such as mango and raspberry will knock your taste buds into tomorrow.

The University of Toronto midtown campus is everything we want in a university: colleges that are straight out of *Masterpiece Theatre*, tranquil courtyards, and noisy playing fields. We may never be college-age again, but we can relive some of the excitement of college life in downtown Toronto.

University of Toronto
walking tours:
June-August:
Monday-Friday 10:30, 12:30 and 2:30
(416) 978-5000

WATERFRONT
Harbour Lights

The story of Toronto is the story of a waterfront. The natural harbour, protected from the worst of the Great Lakes gales by a peninsula (now Toronto Island), has attracted Indians, explorers, navies and merchants for centuries. But too many Torontonians are cut off from the lake by roadways and massive buildings. Take time to explore the exciting world at the water's edge and see the city from an entirely different point of view.

Today's trip begins at the Canadian National Exhibition (CNE) grounds and travels the lakeshore to the foot of Yonge Street. The trip can be driven or it can be easily biked by following the Martin Goodman Recreational Trail, a 20-kilometre ribbon of asphalt and concrete that follows the shoreline from the Humber River to the Beaches. (The portion travelled today is about half that distance.)

The Marine Museum is located on the CNE grounds. Begin a visit with the slide show on the development of Toronto harbour from the days of fur traders, through industrial revolution, to its present status as a "post-industrial" harbour. It is interesting to see how the original wooded shoreline has changed to reflect events both in the city and in the world at large, with wartime, peacetime and modern technology making their mark on the harbour.

A large fleet of model ships on display includes birchbark canoes, York boats, warships and modern container vessels. See a mock-up of a ship's wireless room and find out how early Canadian wireless operators and police co-operated in the capture of a famous criminal in 1910. And of course the museum chronicles the remarkable career of Ned Hanlan, Toronto's own world-champion rower. Remember the days when Toronto was a port of call for luxurious cruise liners.

If it's time for a meal, try the restaurant at the Marine Museum. If not, head across the pedestrian bridge to Ontario Place. You must pay admission to the park in order to tour Canada's illustrious warship, the Tribal Class destroyer HMCS *Haida*. During the summer, visitors may tour the *Haida* with the help of a self-guiding brochure; the remainder of the year the *Haida* is used for training sea cadets. The brochure interprets every inch of the *Haida*, from guns and torpedo tubes to mess deck, captain's sea cabin and the bridge. Find out how 230 sailors live in cramped quarters, pack uniforms and toiletries into a duffel bag, and eat at a table that is in constant motion.

You may want to spend some time visiting Ontario Place. It is a cultural and leisure centre spread over 38 hectares of islands and lagoons. The geodesic dome is the Cinesphere; the six-storey screen is ideal for IMAX films that present a pilot's-eye view of the world, with you (and your innards) swooping over every cliff. If the legendary *North of Superior* is showing while you visit, don't leave without seeing it: this breathtaking picture of Ontario's northern beauty is an excellent way to show off the province to visitors. (The Cinesphere remains open during the winter, unlike the rest of the park.)

The Children's Village at Ontario Place is the best of the best in playgrounds, the first of its kind in North America. A huge covered area has play equipment (safe and supervised) for kids from toddlers to teens, and an outdoor water play area has kids running through waterfalls and sliding down carpeted rapids—a great place on a hot day. The Forum amphitheatre hosts special events from rock to symphony, from dance to kids' performers. The matinees are popular with those who like to brown bag it with their music. Forum shows are included in the Ontario Place admission fee. The Waterfall Showplace stage hosts dance bands Saturday evenings. Ontario Place also has restaurants, water rides and boat rentals.

Now drive or bike east towards Toronto's Harbourfront area and explore what the Marine

Interior, Queen's Quay at Harbourfront

Exterior, Queen's Quay at Harbourfront

Museum calls a "post-industrial" harbour. Parking is located throughout the area; prices vary. Harbourfront is 5 kilometres of waterfront for walking, shopping, dining and special exhibitions. It is organized into six quays (west to east): Bathurst, Spadina, Maple Leaf West, Maple Leaf East, John and York. Begin in the west with the Bathurst quay area and the Toronto Island Airport ferry dock. The action in the water and airspace of the western gap provides some of the best entertainment around: an intricate ballet of helicopters, planes, sailboats and ferries that grows more hectic each summer.

Harbourfront's Sportfishing Centre is at Spadina Quay. If you fancy wrestling with a 20-kilogram salmon (chinook or coho), this is the point of departure for charters. The Harbourfront Antique Market is near the foot of Spadina Avenue and is open daily except Mondays. It is not hard to believe that this is Canada's largest antique fair; there are scores of dealers (over 200 on Sunday) carrying first-rate European and Canadian furniture, glass, china, fine art and heritage clothing. Simply not to be missed.

Next on an eastbound route are the two Maple Leaf quays. There is a public sailing centre where you can sign up for lessons in boating and sailing. Here, too, is the ship used to train commercial divers, the *Fuel Marketer*.

As you tour Harbourfront you'll notice the interesting mix of housing; there are exclusive hotels and condominiums, rent-geared-to-income apartments, and housing for seniors. Many of the buildings are the result of award-winning designs by architects such as Arthur Erikson and the Zeidler Partnership. More housing is planned for the future.

At John Quay the density of tourists and activity picks up. There are three restaurants here. Choose from the Chinese Junk, Wallymagoo's Marinebar, or the Pier 4 Storehouse restaurant. Seafood takes centre stage at Pier 4, Wally's has finger foods, and the Junk offers dim sum lunches. The Hotel Admiral also has several places to eat. John Quay is the place for boaters. Just south of the hotel is the Metro Police Marine Unit, an uncommon collection of rescue and patrol craft. The Nautical Mind bookstore has nautical charts and guides for everywhere

you'd want to explore; it also sells a multitude of books for boatbuilders, navy men and waterside philosophers. The Dock Shoppe is filled to the gunnels with rope fenders, navigational equipment, fashionable boating attire and decorator items for the home deck.

A commonly photographed site at Harbourfront is the Amsterdam Bridge connecting John Quay with York Quay. During the day the bridge is a good vantage point for viewing luxurious yachts, and at night the bridge twinkles with hundreds of tiny lights.

York Quay is a busy place. Check in at the York Quay Centre for complete info on the kaleidoscope of happenings at Harbourfront. The Centre houses open craft studios where you may catch potters, glass blowers and ceramicists at work. The theatres in the York Quay Centre offer free films, concerts and readings, with Sunday being the busiest day. As for events, a small sample includes boat shows, trampoline festivals, gardening displays and fireworks competitions. If all this has you wishing for something simple, the pond behind York Centre turns into a winter skating rink, the only place to skate and enjoy great scenery at the same time.

Heading east, the Power Plant art gallery has changing exhibits of contemporary art and often has activities for kids during the summer and on weekends year-round (closed Mondays). The Power Plant was originally just that, providing energy for the ice-making plant next door; that building is now the DuMaurier Theatre. The waterfront just behind the Power Plant is the location for several tour companies offering harbour cruises on a variety of vessels, such as a 1910 paddle-wheeler and a three-masted schooner. Some of the tours include lunch or dinner.

York Quay contains an impeccably renovated building, Queen's Quay Terminal. This was a gargantuan 1920s warehouse cooled by the ice made next door. It was the first Canadian building constructed of poured concrete. It now has a second life as a shopping centre (almost 100 exclusive boutiques offering everything from bonsai plants to designer hair ribbon), as well as office and apartment space. Queen's Quay Terminal also houses the Premier Dance Theatre, which holds an international dance festival each September.

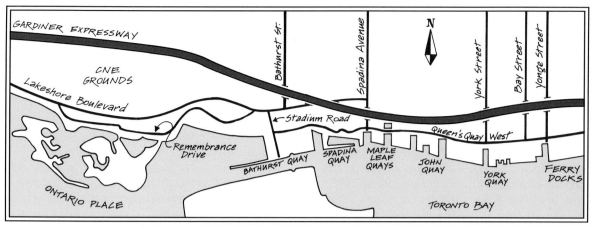

Toronto Waterfront

And if wandering along the waterfront hasn't been enough exercise, join the Queen's Quay Terminal walking program. The terminal is open from 7:30 AM to 9:30 PM and has a measured course for those serious about their regimen. And while we're talking about exercise, one of the best ways to get around Harbourfront is by bike. Rentals are at the intersection of Queen's Quay and Bay Street.

Continue walking east past the Harbour Castle Hotel (the rooftop restaurant is the place for Sunday brunch with a view). If you want to end the day at a unique eating spot, try Captain John's restaurant, a Yugoslavian cruise ship now permanently moored at Harbourfront. The Sunday brunch is especially good (lots of seafood) and the service attentive.

There's nothing like a day spent at Toronto's waterfront. Whether you are a sailor, a jogger or a shopper, you'll find the air refreshing, the view endless and the pace relaxing.

Marine Museum
Monday-Saturday 9:30-5:00
Sundays & Holidays 12:00-5:00
(416) 392-6827

Ontario Place
Mid-May to Labour Day:
Daily 10:00am-1:00am
(416) 965-7711 (recorded message)
(416) 965-7917

HMCS *Haida*
Mid-May to Labour Day:
Daily 10:00-7:00
(416) 965-7917
(416) 965-6331

Harbourfront
Antique Market
Tuesday-Friday 11:00-5:00
Saturday 10:00-5:00
Sunday 8:00-6:00
(416) 340-8377

The Craft Studio
Daily 10:00-6:00
(416) 973-4963

Power Plant Art Gallery
Tuesday-Saturday 12:00-8:00
Sundays & Holidays 12:00-6:00
(416) 973-4949

Harbour Activity Information
(416) 973-3000

DOWNTOWN
Banker's Hours

Many Torontonians think of the city's financial district as the private realm of bankers and lawyers, a little off limits to the ordinary citizen. But an exploration of Bay Street between King and Queen streets reveals a wealth of fine art, some glorious buildings, an underground city and a visitor-friendly stock exchange.

The offices of the five major Canadian banks are clustered together near King and Bay, and each of these modern tower-and-plaza complexes is worth an investigation. The towers are colour-coded: the sleek black towers are the Toronto-Dominion Bank; the red-marble trapezoid, the Bank of Nova Scotia; the dazzling gold boxes (yes, 7,000 kilograms of real gold) are the Royal Bank; the white-marble complex, the Bank of Montreal; and the glass-and-stainless-steel towers, the Canadian Imperial Bank of Commerce.

Some very interesting art decorates each of these office complexes. Ask at the information desk located in the foyer of each bank for a guide to their collection. The T-D Inuit art collection is well worth seeing. Also within the T-D complex, on the lawn near Wellington Street, lie seven bronze cows, a delightful work by Joe Fafard which lends a palpable sense of serenity to the hectic scene. The Royal Bank contains two of Toronto's favourite works. In the foyer hang thousands of gold-and-white metal rods (a sculpture by Jesus Raphael Soto), while along the outside staircase on Front Street, life-size figures battle the wind.

Visit Canadian banking in its finest hour in the 1931 Bank of Commerce building, now part of Commerce Court (southeast corner of King and Bay). Magnificent hardly begins to describe the heavy solid-stone base which rises like a tiered cake to a heavenly height. It is in the banking hall, a dazzling mosaic of gold and blue high above and a reverent hush all around, that one finds the closest thing to a religious experience in the financial district.

Walk outside to Commerce Court. During the summer this courtyard and the one within the T-D centre are good spots to listen to music, have a picnic lunch, and observe the latest office romances. During the winter, high winds make this entire area dangerous. Locals head underground and the wise tourist follows their example. An underground labyrinth with hundreds of shops, services and restaurants connects Union Station to City Hall on Queen Street—truly a city within a city. The section beneath First Canadian Place (Bank of Montreal) contains a marketplace with everything you need for a brown-bag lunch. For classier dining, the best choice is the Fifty-Fourth Dining Room in the Toronto-Dominion Bank. The view of the lake and the CN Tower is unparalleled and the food expertly prepared. (Reservations suggested; closed Sunday.)

Head to the Nova Scotia building on the north side of King Street. The cool marble interior of the Scotia is designed in a style known as Moderne, characterized by a clean and spare look. Notice that the carvings in the banking hall and inside the entrances illustrate the history of the corporation, its maritime connections and role in national development.

Wander (above ground) through the Bay Street "canyon" to appreciate the lovely Art Deco skyscrapers of the 1920s and '30s. Enter the Canada Permanent Building at 320 Bay (1928). Everything that doesn't breathe is covered with lustrous metal: vault doors, mail slots, desks. The elevator doors are especially good; they have figures holding a model of the former Canada Permanent headquarters. Don't miss two beautiful exteriors, the Concourse Building (1928) at the corner of Bay and Adelaide and the Sterling Tower (1928) at the corner of Bay and Richmond. Both buildings have designs that emphasize strong vertical lines and have lots of ornamental work around street-level windows and entranceways. The Concourse entrance

Toronto's business district

features a mosaic designed by Group of Seven artist J.E.H. MacDonald and his son Thoreau.

The last official stop of the day is the Stock Exchange, located in First Canadian Place (Bank of Montreal). The visitors' area displays larger-than- life modern art works and a copy of the frieze that decorates the original stock exchange building (324 Bay Street). That frieze was designed by Charles Comfort and illustrates workers in industries traded on the exchange.

Forty-five-minute exchange tours are offered weekday afternoons that will intrigue even the business neophyte. The polished tour combines commentary and a slide show to explain the development and workings of the Toronto Exchange, the third largest in the world and the most advanced in technological terms. The guide will familiarize you with stocks, bonds, futures, indices, tickers and traders. Now you are ready to observe the action on the "floor" of the exchange. Traders, wearing the colours of their firm (red, green, or even yellow-and-black plaid), meet at each post to negotiate trades. An electronic notice board gives up-to-the-minute news from major centres around the world; this is the best place to stay informed in Toronto.

It is said that Toronto's business *is* business. Fortunately for the daytripper, that business environment also provides for a pleasant day of lovely buildings and fine art.

Toronto Stock Exchange
Monday-Friday 9:30-4:00
Tours 2:00
(416) 947-4700

The Fifty-Fourth Dining Room
(416) 366-6576

WATERFRONT
Islands in the Sun

Sometimes you need to get away from it all, escape to where nobody knows you, to have a breeze ruffle your hair. And sometimes you want to be where the action is, hear the midway, rub shoulders with fellow pleasure-seekers. Sound like an ad for a Caribbean resort? Well, put your wallet back in your pocket, for such a perfect escape exists just a ferry ride away, on the Toronto Islands.

Often referred to as "The Island," there are actually several islands—Centre, Ward's, Algonquin, South, Muggs and Olympic are the largest—interconnected by walkways, so a day can be spent enjoying the unique character of each. Ferries leave from the foot of Bay Street behind the Harbour Castle Hotel and travel to Ward's Island, Centre Island and Hanlan's Point (only Ward's Island and Hanlon's Point during the winter). Ferries operate frequently from early morning to late at night. Be sure to call the recorded message for exact times, which vary seasonally.

Let's start where the action is: Centre Island. Have you noticed that everyone in Toronto

disappears on a hot weekend? You will find many of them on Centre Island, so plan a visit very early in the morning or midweek. Centreville, a 7-hectare amusement park, is geared to the very young; in fact, at this delightful place the height limits restrict *tall* riders, not short ones. There are pony rides, boat rides, a water flume, bumper cars, games of chance and food stands. Far Enough Farm has a goodly assortment of animals craving a pat. The whole family will enjoy renting a canoe, paddle boat or rowboat for a few hours of patrolling the lagoons and bays of Centre Island. While there is lots of picnicking on Centre Island, quieter spots are on nearby Olympic Island, which also offers extraordinary views of the Toronto skyline.

Centre Island also has formal gardens and fountains, wading pools (the ones in the garden area appear cleanest), and bike rentals (not only bikes built for two, but quadracycles for two and four). There's a beach on the Lake Ontario side. Be warned: the water is very cold and sometimes polluted. A visit to Centre Island isn't complete without seeing

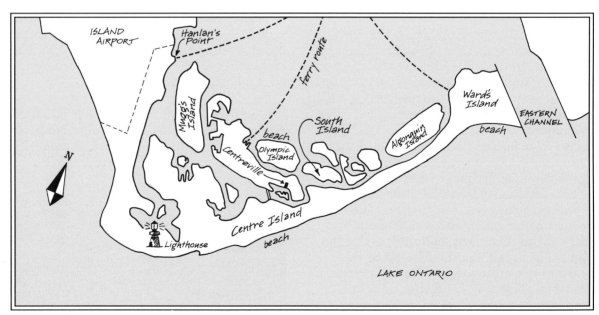

Toronto Islands

St. Andrew's by the Sea. This charming building is shared by Anglican and Roman Catholic congregations and has beautiful stained-glass windows. No wonder it is a popular wedding spot for both islanders and yacht-club families.

Centre Island has two ferry landings. The ferry called the Centre Island ferry lands near Centreville and the other active areas on the island. The Hanlon's Point ferry landing is located at the west end of Centre Island. A free trackless train runs between the two ferry docks. (If the Centre Island ferries are lined up, catch a Hanlan's ferry and then take the train to the main part of Centre Island.) The train passes the 1808 Gibraltar Point lighthouse (haunted by a former keeper murdered by rowdy sailors) and more swimming beaches. Behind the water filtration plant is a natural area (closed to the public during bird breeding season) which is considered the best place on the continent to see saw-whet owls (October and November are best). Muggs Island is also a favourite with birders, since it has a colony of black-crowned night herons, one of Ontario's most unusual-looking birds.

There's lots to do at Hanlan's Point. There is a bike-rental stand. The trout pond is so well stocked that success is almost guaranteed (bring your own equipment). Hanlan's Point is sailor country. With three very exclusive yacht clubs and a public marina, the water teems with boats large and small, all side-stepping each other and the ferries. There's also entertainment in the air, the airspace over the Island Airport being almost as crowded as the waters of the bay.

If city life is getting you down, a day on Ward's and Algonquin islands is a choice antidote. Hike or bike from Centre Island (45 minutes by foot) or take the Ward's Island ferry from the dock. These islands are separated from the action by acres of secluded parkland and North America's only Frisbee golf course (participants appear quite dedicated, carrying around large bags of discs for tossing into basket targets). The waterways are enchanting, with overhanging willows, arched wooden bridges and weather-worn tugs that look like old salts when compared with the sleek yachts in the bay.

The 250 or so homes on Ward's and Algonquin islands are cherished remainders of the large recreational community that thrived on the islands from the time of World War I. The metropolitan government demolished the Centre Island homes to make way for parkland. (It is unlikely that the councillors predicted the two decades of anguish and struggle required to preserve the remaining island homes.) There is a strong sense of community among the islanders, some of whom have chosen to live out entire lives here. It does appear to be a perfectly idyllic life, judging from a slow stroll along the island laneways. There is an unusual assortment of homes, some spacious and fashionable in design, others tiny and in disrepair. But the atmosphere is restful and pleasant, and the fantastic Toronto skyline is just waiting for the photographer (sunset can be spectacular for photos).

The Toronto Islands give the daytripper a wider choice of activities than anywhere else in southern Ontario. With the amazingly low cost of a return ferry ride, the Islands are a great travel bargain. Good thing, because you will want to return often.

Island Ferries
Daily, usually every 20 or 30 minutes
from 6:30 am to 11:30 pm
(416) 392-8193 (recorded message)

Centreville
May-September, daily
September-Thanksgiving, weekends

Island Information
(416) 392-8186
(416) 367-8193

14

DOWNTOWN
Street Legal

Street Legal, the popular television series, chronicles life within a small Queen Street West law office, a life full of unusual characters, backroom deals, steamy romance and beautiful settings. Can this be the real life of lawyers? You be the judge on this exploration of Toronto's legal district.

Any tour concerning the law must begin at Osgoode Hall, located at the corner of Queen Street and University Avenue. Osgoode served as a law school for over a century, and it currently houses both the Supreme Court of Ontario and the Law Society of Upper Canada, the governing body of the legal profession in Ontario. Osgoode is one of Toronto's most familiar landmarks and its green sward is a welcome oasis in the concrete desert. Massive

columned entrances and a formal wrought-iron fence seem designed to keep visitors at bay, yet Osgoode Hall is open to the public and tours are offered weekdays during the summer. (Legend has it that the fence was a nineteenth-century guard against cattle. A class of law students put the cattle gates to the test, and indeed a cow cannot pass through.)

Enter Osgoode via the centre-block doors. This is a world of Latin terminology and black robes, prestige and privilege. The hour-long tour, led by a law clerk, includes several courtrooms replete with pastel plasterwork and massive judges' benches. You may get a look at the bullet holes resulting from an attack during a trial. From the wild 1800s? No, they date to 1986. The highlight of the

Osgoode Hall with City Hall in background

tour is the romantic Great Library which features shelves of law books rising 10 metres, a twisting iron staircase and windows etched with Victoria's monogram.

So far everything you've seen is open to the public. But the Osgoode tour includes the inner sanctums of the Law Society of Upper Canada. You are on sacred ground, for only Law Society "benchers" and tour members are allowed in this area. Lounges and meeting rooms look much as they have looked for generations, with pens and ink lying at the ready for the next meeting. The tour concludes with a visit to the Law Society museum. Artifacts, historic documents and office furnishings describe the development of the Ontario court system and its British heritage.

The private operations of the Law Society have been laid bare before us. But where does the law meet the people? In two places close to Osgoode. The first is Provincial Court at 361 University Avenue, just north of Osgoode Hall. The courtrooms are open to the public, but a check-in with the guards might be a good idea.

A second, more lively face of the law is seen at the Old City Hall on Queen Street at Bay, which is now used as a courthouse. This is another grand piece of architecture, with ornamental glass and mosaic tile everywhere; and yet the atmosphere is dramatically different from the quiet dignity of Osgoode. Giggling newlyweds, fresh from the justice of the peace, pose for photos; scores of families, fidgety or patient, wait for cases in the young offenders department; people of all sorts float in and out of the foyer, fighting traffic tickets or buying licences.

Exit Old City Hall and walk west along Queen Street to University Avenue. The dignified red-brick building on the northwest corner of the intersection is Campbell House, home to Sir William Campbell, Chief Justice of Upper Canada from 1825 to 1829 and the first Canadian judge knighted. Campbell would have presided over many of the most publicized cases of the day.

Campbell House is a beautiful Georgian building, its formal appearance relieved by a charming semi-circular porch and a large fanlight over the entrance. Costumed guides provide informative tours of the home,

painting a detailed picture of life upstairs and downstairs in high society during the 1820s.

Don't miss the leather water buckets standing behind the front door. Toronto, like most other nineteenth-century towns, was plagued by fire; perhaps that is why Campbell House was one of the first homes built of brick.

As a judge in the backwater of Upper Canada, Campbell was intimately aware of the need for a local base for legal education. At the time, most lawyers and judges were trained in Britain (Campbell himself never studied law), and many found life on the frontier too challenging and poor-paying to keep them on this side of the Atlantic. Campbell spearheaded the campaign for a law school in Upper Canada, and beautiful Osgoode Hall was the result.

It's probably time for a meal. If you care to dine overlooking the gargoyles of Old City Hall, the best view is from across the street at the City View Café on the 8th floor of the Bay (formerly Simpsons). For a more adventurous menu, try any of the bistros and restaurants along Queen Street West, a short walk west of Campbell House. Not only is this the best eating district in town, but if you walk as far west as number 280, you'll see the building that is, in television land, the office of Leon and the gang from *Street Legal*.

Take a day to explore Toronto's world of lawyers and courtrooms. While television's romance and petty intrigue may be pure fiction, there is no doubt that the legal district along Queen Street provides one of the most beautiful backdrops in town.

Osgoode Hall (tours)
July & August:
Monday-Friday 1:00
(416) 947-3300

Campbell House
mid-May to mid-October:
Daily 12:00-5:00
mid-October to mid-May:
Monday-Friday 9:30-12:00 and 2:30-5:00
(416) 597-0227

DOWNTOWN
It's Christmastime in the City

No matter where you celebrate it, Christmas will always be a magical mix of religion, romance and nostalgia. Toronto puts together a Christmas season complete with twinkling lights, moonlight skating, roasting chestnuts and even the star of Bethlehem.

It's easy to get caught up in the rat race of holiday buying, baking and partying, and to forget the original cause of the celebration. Get back to the basics and the beginnings of Christmas by taking in the Star of Bethlehem show at the McLaughlin Planetarium. (The planetarium is just south of the Royal Ontario Museum at Bloor and Queen's Park Crescent; Museum subway stop.)

The Star of Bethelem show (screened only during December and January) takes the viewer back 2,000 years and south 15 degrees latitude, recreating the night skies over Bethlehem around the time of the first Noël. Visitors recline in theatre seats and watch as stars, planets, wisemen, kings and other Christmas story characters are projected on the domed ceiling. The narrator describes the search through ancient texts and the use of astronomical projections (*backwards* in time) to pinpoint unusual conditions that may have given rise to the star of Bethlehem. Without spoiling the conclusion of this enlightening and enjoyable show, be assured that there is a scientific basis for the story of the star of Bethlehem. (And the rest, as they say, is history.)

Christmas traditions vary from culture to culture, and from one age to the next. Savour the festive spirit of the Victorian age at Mackenzie House, the modest home of rebel and mayor William Lyon Mackenzie, located at 82 Bond Street. (Exit at the Dundas subway stop, then walk east two blocks and south to number 82.)

Although the Victorians enjoyed low-key Christmas celebrations, Mackenzie House projects a charmingly festive spirit. Learn how British holiday traditions were translated to suit local conditions. For example, since holly and ivy are too delicate to grow in Ontario, Mackenzie House is festooned with cranberries and popcorn. See a cedar kissing bough and gifts typical of the era (such as dolls, tops and needle books). The aroma of cinnamon and wood smoke fill the house, and visitors are invited to the basement kitchen for "jumble" cookies, shortbread, spiced cider and fruit tarts with homemade preserves. And although Christmas cards were not yet the fashion, you can visit the printing press at Mackenzie House to have your name printed on a holiday greeting. Good Scots, the Mackenzies celebrated Hogmannay, or New Year's, with more gusto than Christmas, so that Mackenzie House remains full of good cheer and festive activities for the whole family well into January.

Back to the spirit of Christmas present. Time to enjoy a vigorous skate in the out of doors. Toronto has several downtown rinks, each with its own unique character. Just northwest of Mackenzie House at the corner of Victoria and Gould is the Ryerson Polytechnical Institute rink, where you can skate amid gigantic granite boulders, a consummate backdrop for the Canadian pastime. Good rink for beginners.

Walk to Yonge Street and the Eaton Centre. Don't join the frenzy in the stores, but use the mall as a convenient way of walking south. The Eaton Centre is a good place to pick up lunch on today's trip. A number of the eateries here are outlets of chains particular to Toronto, such as Toby's Good Eats (two-fisted burgers), Magic Pan (crêpes) and Lime Rickey's (50s diner).

Another good reason for visiting the Eaton Centre at Christmas is the larger-than-life decorations. Although the display changes each year, it is guaranteed to impress. The mall is open after the stores close, and also on Sundays. Perhaps Toronto's most conspicuous Christmas decorations are the windows at the Bay (Simpsons) store on Queen Street. At one

Skating at City Hall

time, both Eaton's and Simpsons had glamorous displays facing Queen Street. Alas, we must now content ourselves with the Bay displays, which are always lavish, animated and spirited. Even a Scrooge would be amused.

Continue west along Queen to the most popular skating rink downtown, Nathan Phillips Square in front of the "new" City Hall. The rink is a swirl of colour all day and well into the night, when a zillion coloured lights twinkle from trees along Queen and between Osgoode Hall and City Hall. There are few more romantic spots in Toronto—sure beats the local community arena. If you have left eating until now, visit the sidewalk vendors for a hotdog or roasted chestnuts.

Spending a day in Toronto during the Christmas season is like re-living a day of childhood. Marvel at animated window displays, see the star of Bethlehem, have cider and cookies, and skate under the stars. A Merry Christmas to all and to all a good night!

Royal Ontario Museum
Holiday hours vary, so
phone to check schedule
(416) 586-5549

DOWNTOWN
The Game is Afoot

If you love crime stories, whether cops and robbers or espionage and intrigue, then Toronto's the city for you. Spend a day in the world of skullduggery by investigating a museum, a reference library and a specialty bookshop all dedicated to bringing out the sleuth in you.

Begin at the Metropolitan Toronto Police Museum and Discovery Centre located in the impressive new police headquarters at 44 College Street (a short walk from the College subway stop). Through exhibits and interactive games, the museum covers four topics: the history of the Toronto force, investigative techniques, modern policing and a 1929 police station.

There's a lot of Toronto history here, and long-time residents will enjoy perusing photographs and memorabilia from past decades, including ample material on Toronto's most famous crimes cases. None could be more exciting than that of the notorious Boyd gang. During 1951 and 1952 a gang of bank robbers, led by Toronto-born Edwin Alonzo Boyd, committed many hold-ups in the city, made a couple of daring and ingenious escapes from jail, and gunned down police officers. The full story, including photographs and newspaper articles, makes for a captivating display.

Exercise your grey matter by distinguishing between real and counterfeit currency and jewellery. Or follow the history of identification from the early Bertillon system (identifying people from measurements of little fingers, left ears and other body parts) through the science of fingerprinting, to photography and DNA printing.

For kids (and grown-ups) intrigued by the glamour of police work, there's information on the mounted and motorcycle units, and displays on police recruitment standards. The weapons display includes standard items such as guns (real and fake) and knives, as well as less conventional weapons such as pantyhose and scarves. Other exhibits cover police auxiliaries, women on the force, street drugs, historic police vehicles and emergency aid.

Arthur Conan Doyle Room

Although there are a small number of temporary displays in the lobby of the police headquarters, the museum does not open until early 1993. Don't be disappointed; wait until after the official opening to visit.

Your next assignment, should you decide to accept it, is lunch. There's no doubt that British crime writers have made a permanent mark on detective and espionage literature, so where better to lunch than at the Hop and Grape pub on College Street just west of Yonge. Somerset cheddar pie, beef and Guiness stew, and cockie leekie soup will fill you up in a friendly atmosphere. While there is a full slate of beer on tap, like Younger's Tartan or Smithwick's, there's also ginger beer and orange pekoe tea for those who want to keep their heads clear for the work at hand.

Ride the Yonge Street subway northbound and exit at Bloor. Walk north on Yonge to the Metropolitan Toronto Reference Library. Once on the Language and Literature floor ask to see the Arthur Conan Doyle Room. Considered the best collection of material by and on Conan Doyle and Sherlock Holmes in the world, this room is a must-see for any devotee of modern detection literature. The room is decorated as Holmes would have left it, complete with Victorian calling cards from characters in the stories, worn Persian rug, pipes and tobacco, and even the infamous cocaine needle.

The highlight of the collection is the original Sherlock Holmes stories in all their editions and translations. The collection includes over 200 editions of *The Sign of Four* alone, in all its variation of binding and print, including one version in Pitman shorthand. Holmesian or not, you'll be delighted by the collection's *Strand Magazine*, in which the first 58 stories appeared. The excellent illustrations accompanying the stories have shaped our vision of the detective almost as much as Doyle's words.

Students of literature appreciate the extensive resources of the Arthur Conan Doyle Room. There is a large section on literary criticism, including imitations and satires on the writings of Doyle. Lastly, the collection covers Doyle himself, his remarkable career and interests, such as the occult, sport and medicine.

After gaining an appreciation for how one set of detective stories could become such an integral part of our culture, you may well be hankering to spin a few crime yarns of your own. Return to the Yonge Street subway line and ride north to Davisville. Either hop on a Bayview bus or walk east to Bayview and *The Sleuth of Baker Street* at number 1595 (located between Davisville and Eglinton).

The glory of this bookshop is the completeness of its offerings. Whether you lean to cold-war spy tales or Dick Tracy, you'll find reading material to last a lifetime in just one store— and a knowledgeable staff that can quickly put their fingers on just what you're searching for. For the junior gumshoe, there's a large section just for kids, filled with books on adventures at school and on holiday, as well as volumes of three-minute mysteries and crime detection experiments.

Literary hopefuls should check out the section on detection writing, especially the guides to dialogue, characterization, setting, themes, and so on. Especially helpful is *The Writer's Complete Crime Reference Book*, which will give your writing an air of authenticity, from how much arsenic is needed to kill off the victim to correct police terminology. There are also guides to finding a publisher or self-publication.

It's time to don the deerstalker, flag a hansom cab and speed home, fully equipped to add your own mark to the work of crime fiction.

Metro Toronto Police Museum & Discovery Centre
Daily, 24 hours
(416) 324-2222

Metro Toronto Reference Library
Arthur Conan Doyle Room
Tuesday, Friday and Saturday
2:00-4:00
Wednesday 6:00-8:00
(416) 393-7000

Sleuth of Baker Street
Daily, including Sundays
(416) 483-3111

DOWNTOWN
The Best Seat in the House

The twinkle of marquee lights, the hush just before the curtain rises, the thrill of a perfect performance. Where would big-city life be without the magic of the theatre? Life in Toronto is brighter these days, thanks to a stellar cast of new and reborn theatres—the Pantages, the Elgin and Winter Garden, and Roy Thompson Hall. You don't need to spend big bucks to attend these halls. Public tours give visitors a chance to appreciate these grand beauties, as well as provide a rare peek backstage that is not offered patrons in the box seats.

Public tours (provided at a modest cost) vary according to performance schedules, so be sure to phone and check times. In general, the Pantages and the Elgin and Winter Garden theatres offer tours on Saturday mornings and at least one weekday (morning or late afternoon). Roy Thompson Hall offers midday tours every day but Sunday. It may be possible to view all three sites in one day, with a little subway scrambling, or your theatre tour may be spread over two days.

If you can visit the interior of only one theatre, make it the Pantages (263 Yonge Street, Dundas subway stop). Constructed in 1919, the Pantages was the largest vaudeville house in the British Empire. This may look like a marble showroom, but the building itself is actually a hollow plaster palace. Scagliola, the art of applying plaster dust and binder, followed by hand-painted veining, is executed so well that you'll need to knock the pillars to believe that they are indeed plaster and not marble. The Yonge Street foyer is truly one of Toronto's marvels, the lavish white plasterwork on clear, bright pastels making the space seem like a piece of Wedgwood china. (A foyer like this makes waiting in line worthwhile.) The unusual steep staircase to the lobby is actually a walkway connecting the tiny Yonge entrance with the main theatre space on Victoria; that way, the owners could have two marquees and doorways while keeping the space on expensive but more visible Yonge Street tiny.

Restoration work was based on historic photographs, thousands of paint and fabric samples, and building drawings. Old-timers gasp when they see how flawlessly the new decor and ambience mimics the original. The Pantages is home to the *Phantom of the Opera*, which will play until 1993. The stage is perfect for such an extravaganza, for it is larger than most stages, at 30 metres by 10 metres. The spirited tour (itself a good piece of theatre) includes a question period on the technical wizardry of the performance. Don't worry, this is handled in a way that doesn't spoil the show. In fact, you can't tour this landmark without pining for tickets.

If it's time for a lunch break, the only spot to consider is the Senator on Victoria Street right across from the Pantages. Supplying the ultimate in diner ambience, the Senator has been cherished by downtowners for over 40 years. The menu ranges from kippers on challah toast to genuine macaroni and cheese, to an eclectic array of desserts such as peach-pecan pie, bread pudding or Phantom's Delight (a melange including devil's chocolate and raspberry tartufo). The Senator is rich in theatre posters, swivel stools, arborite tabletops and the smoothest service in the Little Apple. Always busy, with a clientele as varied as the menu.

South of the Pantages are the Elgin and Winter Garden theatres, the only operating "stacked" theatres left in the world (189 Yonge, just north of Queen). By building one theatre on top of another, the owners (originally the Loew's vaudeville chain) could reap greater profits from the expensive Yonge Street property. The result is a theatre building spanning seven storeys from lowest excavation to rooftop. These two theatres are as unlike the Pantages as vaudeville is unlike opera, and yet they were the product of the same architect, Thomas Lamb of New York.

The tour begins in the Yonge Street foyer, a dazzling display of gilding, mirrors and marble.

Wintergarden Theatre

Elgin Theatre

Lobby of the Elgin Theatre

Don't ask where the show begins—it obviously begins here. Exacting standards in historical restoration were set by the Ontario Heritage Foundation, even to the extent that a spelling mistake in the list of composers that decorates the lobby was discovered but left uncorrected. See if you can spot it. The opulence of the lobby doesn't disappoint, for the Elgin Theatre is ashimmer with gilded carvings and red-and-gold wall coverings. The light fixtures, each with thousands of sparkling beads, represent hours of volunteer time. Five levels of cascading lobbies are hung with the original vaudeville scenery backdrops, satin painted with fabric dye and diamond dust. This is part of the largest collection of these properties in existence. Take time to examine the elevators.

They are straight out of the old flicks and are among the few still operated by hand.

The Winter Garden Theatre. The name says it all: this magical setting does look like a garden in winter, complete with tree-trunk pillars, thousands of real Ontario beech branches hanging from the ceiling, and multi-coloured garden lanterns. The trelliswork and branches decorating the walls are the original paint; renovators simply removed 70 years of accumulated grime. The acoustics in the Winter Garden are so superior that there has been no need to add a speaker system.

The Elgin and Winter Garden theatres also house a theatre museum, and tour guests are allowed backstage to see the original equipment used for operating sets, lighting and curtains. There is a vaudevillian dressing room, a tiny cubbyhole shared by several performers. Artifacts include costumes, make-up, steamer trunks and gaslights. The warmth from the lights was used to heat not only grease paint but also baby bottles, since many female performers had their babies with them.

Roy Thompson Hall is the contemporary member of Toronto's theatreland. Designed by Arthur Erickson, the hall's critics liken it to a glass muffin set upside down. But the critics are silenced (quite literally) by the marvellously successful interior: the acoustics are among the very best in the world. Tour guides demonstrate the echo-free acoustics during the tour. The search for perfect sound influenced every aspect of the hall's design, such as the lack of aisles (for sound to get lost in) and the acrylic disks and fabric banners that can be moved when necessary to alter the arrangement of the hall. The monochromatic colour scheme—concrete, chrome and grey— focuses attention on the performers and the audience. The theory worked, for although a newcomer, Roy Thompson Hall is already a favourite place to meet and mingle.

Roy Thompson Hall is home to the Toronto Symphony Orchestra and the Toronto Mendelssohn Choir. But this hall isn't only for the tuxedo set; there is a lively program of musical events designed to make everyone in the community feel welcome. A small sample of activities include a weekend-morning cushion concert series for kids from 4 to 10 years, seniors dance programs, and lunchtime recitals by up-and-coming students and professionals.

Returning outside Roy Thompson Hall, take a gander at the Royal Alexandra Theatre on King Street. It is a fine example of Edwardian architecture inside and out. Unfortunately there are no public tours. But when Ed Mirvish rescued the Royal Alex from the wrecker's ball, he became a major force in reviving theatre throughout the city.

The days of vaudeville and a 15-cent theatre seat are long gone, but for a couple of bucks and a subway token, the daytripper of the 1990s gets to sit in the best seat in the house.

Pantages tours
Monday-Friday 11:30
Saturday 10:30
(416) 362-3218

Elgin and Winter Garden tours
Thursday 5:00
Saturday 11:00
(416) 963-3571

Roy Thompson tours
Monday-Saturday 12:30
(416) 593-4822

NORTH YORK
Kidstuff

Toronto is fertile ground for daytripping families. There are innumerable places geared to kids—feeding, clothing, exercising and entertaining them. But there are two problems: crowds and funds. There is usually too much of the former and too little of the latter. A ready solution lies in making a family excursion away from the crowds to North York, where Gibson House and the Toronto Puppet Centre provide a fun-filled, inexpensive outing.

Historic Gibson House is located on the west side of Yonge Street a few blocks north of Sheppard Avenue. Be on the lookout for the narrow laneway just past Park Home Avenue.

This classic Georgian brick home was constructed in 1851 by David Gibson, a Scots immigrant farmer and land surveyor. Named Willow Dale (a name adopted by the local community), it was the second home for David and Eliza and their seven children, the first having been burned by Loyalist troops during the Rebellion of 1837. After fleeing to the United States as a fugitive, Gibson was eventually pardoned, and he returned to build this home, which is furnished to the mid-1800s period.

History springs into life for children because Gibson House tour guides make a special effort to include them as active participants in

Toronto Puppet Centre

tours, inviting them to feel scratchy wool blankets and lumpy straw mattresses, or asking them what a child's commode chair might by used for. You come away with a clear idea of how children of 1850 might have worked and played, learned, eaten and slept. There are frequent special-event weekends at Gibson House, and many of these are designed especially for children. Kids get a chance to spin wool, do Christmas baking, play old-fashioned games, or make ice cream. An addition to Willow Dale contains changing museum displays on nineteenth-century life, as well as a gift shop with interesting items for kids and grown-ups, such as craft kits, maps and toys.

The tantalizing aromas that emanate from the spacious Gibson House kitchen will serve to whet the family appetite. One of the best bets for travelling families is the Victoria & Albert pub, one of the few restaurants in the area that is open daily. And pub food is terrific kid food—bangers and mash, fish and chips, shepherd's pie. The ample velvet bench seats are tailor-made for squirmy tots and the service is definitely kid-friendly. If you have a family in which each member craves a different style of cuisine, try Maxwell's Mix (open Saturday dinner and all day Sunday). This bistro has a little of everything, from tortillas to teriyaki. A lot of the food is finger food (read fun food), so introduce junior to calamari (it becomes kid food when it's fried and served with yogurt dip) or pita stuffed with shrimp. Both restaurants are on Yonge just south of Gibson House.

And now on to one of Metro's best spots for young kids: the Toronto Puppet Centre. Drive south on Yonge to Avondale Avenue (just north of the 401) and head east four blocks to the Glen Avon Public School, home to the Puppet Centre. And what a perfect environment for a children's theatre, since fountains, coat hooks and washrooms are already sized for children. Kids seem to enjoy sitting on the gym floor, whether their parents join them or choose the folding chairs at the back.

Puppet performances by over four dozen different professional companies run on Tuesdays, Wednesdays, Thursdays and Saturdays from October through June. During the summer, the performances are on weekdays. Tickets are sold at the door, but it's a good idea to pick them up at the box office (open regular business hours), since the Puppet Centre is very popular and the show you want may be sold out.

There is something at the Puppet Centre to suit every family. Some performances are for kids as young as three, others for teens, and some for the whole family. The subject matter is also diverse: folk tales from around the globe, circus-style shows, mysteries and social dramas. Puppetry form varies from familiar hand puppets to marionettes to shadow puppets, and lively audience participation is common. There are also a number of performances in French.

The Puppet Centre is not only a performance place, it is also a museum, studio and training centre. If you thought that all puppets were hand puppets, then you're in for a surprise. The museum contains many varieties of puppets from across Europe and North America, with fascinating text describing the long and honourable puppet theatre tradition. Come face to face with oldies Punch and Judy, as well as media stars such as Hollyhock or the dogs used on Ontario Hydro ads. Kids love the hands-on area of the museum where they are free to experiment with hand, rod and marionette-style puppets on real stages. Glance into the studio, where lifeless foam and fabric may become Ali Baba, Hamlet or even CBC's Mike Duffy.

From learning about children's chores in the nineteenth century to being charmed by a puppet fairy tale, you'll agree that North York has the right stuff—kidstuff.

Toronto Puppet Centre
Monday-Friday 9:00-4:00
Saturday 1:00-3:15
Performance season:
September-June:
Tuesday, Wednesday, Thursday and Saturday
(occasionally on other days)
June-August:
Call for schedule
(416) 222-9029

Gibson House
Tuesday-Friday 9:30-5:00
Saturday, Sunday & Holidays 12:00-5:00
(416) 225-0146

21

DOWNTOWN
Muddy York

Toronto, originally muddy York, has its roots considerably east of what is now downtown, about 1 kilometre east of Yonge. Over the decades the hub of activity crept westward, a mixed blessing for the town, for although years of neglect brought decrepitude, it also protected many of Toronto's earliest buildings from redevelopment. Thus, the history buff can take a walking tour of a complete nineteenth-century town. Take a copy of *Toronto Architecture: A City Guide* with you for informative descriptions of the buildings on today's tour.

An Old Toronto day should begin, appropriately enough, on Toronto Street, the early equivalent of the Bay Street canyon and at one time the most gracious street in town (if going by subway, exit at King and walk east). Number 10 is a Bank of Canada building (1851-53). This Greek Revival building is everything a bank should be: monumental columns, fanlighted Georgian doorway, British arms at the roofline. Across the street is the first Consumers' Gas Company office (1876). This building and the one next to it on the corner (Trust and Loan, 1870) are echoes of Italian palazzi, a style fashionable for serious head offices of the period.

To see where early Torontonians once shopped, walk south on Toronto Street to Colborne. Colborne's old-time atmosphere is due to a narrow roadway and low-rise buildings sited close to the street; one can almost hear the clip-clop of horses' hoofs and the call of newspaper boys. E.J. Lennox, responsible for the Old City Hall, designed many of the shops on Colborne, with his signature of red-sandstone arches above and dark stonework below—unmistakably Toronto.

Head south to Wellington and Front streets and the 1892 Gooderham Building. The Gooderhams were one of York's influential families and this masterpiece was their distilling empire headquarters. It's not a large building, but its weird shape, rich architectural detail and painted west side steal the hearts of Torontonians and visitors alike. The south side of Front Street from Scott to Market presents a prosperous and orderly Victorian face indeed, an entire row of restored buildings which would have been stores on the main floor, and warehouse and office space above. Each warehouse would have had its own loading dock (literally), because at the time of construction they backed onto Lake Ontario.

Head further east along Front to the St. Lawrence Market, which comprises buildings on both sides of Front Street at Jarvis. This square, a farmer's market since the early 1800s, was also the site of the City Hall. The South Market incorporates those old civic chambers of 1845; if you stand among the vendors and look north, the brick exterior of the original City Hall looks down at you. The city chambers are now the Market Gallery (accessible from the front foyer), where the City of Toronto Archives has fascinating displays on the history of the city—not to be missed. The market, with its produce vendors, sandwich bars and bakeries, is the best spot to pick up lunch today.

Walk north to King and Jarvis streets to admire St. Lawrence Hall (1850). This building was most noted for its ornately plastered and chandeliered Great Hall, which fed and entertained Toronto's who's who for much of the 1800s. Return south to Front Street and walk east.

The Young People's Theatre at Frederick Street was originally the stable for the city's streetcar horses (1888). Further east at Berkeley sits the Canadian Opera Company, in some of the most handsome factories anywhere—arched windows, dichromatic brickwork, stepped gables (1882-1904). Continue walking east to Trinity Street. The Gooderham and Worts distillery still stands just south of Front Street, evocative of both the beautiful and beastly faces of nineteenth-century industrial life (1859-1927).

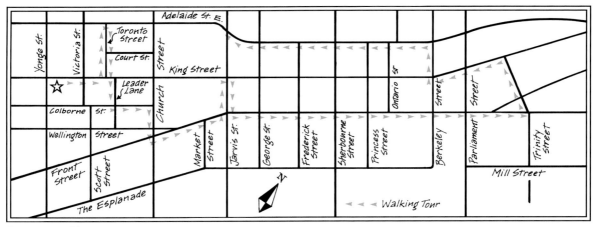

Downtown Toronto

So much for public York. Where did the people toiling in the factories and offices actually live? While bosses lived in mansions along Jarvis, the working poor lived out entire lives in the vicinity of Berkeley and Trinity streets. Walk north on Trinity to the Enoch Turner Schoolhouse, Toronto's oldest standing school (1849). An excellent restoration lets the visitor picture 50 street urchins, complete with slate and chalk, crowded in this room with the Gothic windows (open weekdays). At the corner of Trinity and King stands Little Trinity Church (1843). This "poor man's church" was founded by local industrialists for Irish immigrant workers who could not afford the pew rents at lofty St. James'. The Tudor-style church is quaint outside and very simple inside (much altered since a 1961 fire), and it is open to the public.

Other than the workplace, where did the world of rich and poor meet? Perhaps at the post office. Walk west along King and north on Berkeley, past a row of tiny workingmen's cottages typical of Toronto 100 years ago. At 164 Adelaide East is the 1833 postmaster's house, now the Post Office Museum, with a superb collection of books and maps of early Toronto, and many items of interest to the philatelist. Most of all, this is a fun place for kids, who can use quill pens to write a letter, seal it with wax, and have it hand postmarked. Costumed interpreters create a realistic atmosphere, bemoaning politics and the latest (1830s) gossip.

Everything's up to date in muddy York. This prosperous nineteenth-century town, complete with city hall, banks, factories, church, school and post office, is not a historic re-creation, but is alive and well and waiting to be visited in the St. Lawrence neighbourhood of modern Toronto.

St. Lawrence Market
Tuesday-Thursday 8:00-6:00
Friday 8:00-7:00
Saturday 5:00-5:00
(416) 392-7219

Market Gallery
Wednesday-Friday 10:00-4:00
Saturday 9:00-4:00
Sunday 12:00-4:00
(416) 392-7604

Enoch Turner Schoolhouse
Monday-Friday 9:30-4:30
(416) 863-0010

Post Office Museum
Daily 10:00-4:00
(416) 865-1833

22

DOWNTOWN
East Meets West

Travel guides rhapsodize over Toronto's fascinating neighbourhoods. Two popular destinations are the Beaches (located along Queen Street East) and Queen Street West. It is hard to believe that one street can offer such an engaging contrast in style and that these two neighbourhoods are only a streetcar ride apart. This trip describes a day beginning in the Beaches and winding up on Queen Street West, although it can be travelled in the reverse order.

Board the Queen East streetcar and head for one of Toronto's fashionable addresses, the Beaches. (It is more accurately the Beach, but the Beaches is more commonly used.) Disembark the streetcar near Lee Avenue and tour Kew Gardens, where the area's first settler, Joseph Williams, started a market-garden farm in the mid-1800s. Eventually the holdings were turned into parkland and a resort area for city-weary visitors, many of whom ended up building summer cottages or permanent homes. Although the atmosphere was originally "English seaside resort," the Beaches of today is an enclave for young and newly rich families who are attracted by lakeside parks, proximity to downtown and family-friendly neighbourhoods.

Take a ramble along streets between Queen and the lake, an area of remarkable architectural diversity. Be on the lookout for the original clapboard holiday cottages (especially around Kenilworth), the later mock-Tudor country homes (they are concentrated in the Silverbirch area), and post-1960s renovations (log cabin, stucco, you name it) built by the young professionals who replaced the flower children. Make sure your tour includes the famous lakeside boardwalk, a common subject for photographers.

Beachites love to see and be seen on Queen. The ambience is year-round sporty, with merchants concentrating on smart casual clothing and the restaurants serving either beach burgers or mass-market California food on summer patios meant for people-watching. The teens who hang out here are heavily into skateboards and designer beach wear. Judging by the Queen East scene, life is comfortable just the way it is: comfortably well-off, comfortably relaxed and comfortably conservative.

Some good shopping can be had at Miracles (2014 Queen), with lots of posters and other browsables. Edwards Books and Art (2179) is the place to find beautiful books. The Beaches is kids' turf. If you have small fry, don't miss the Toy Circus (2036), the Kids' Video Store (1924) or Mastermind of the Beaches (1947). If it's time for a meal, the Palm (1959 Queen) is a local legend, serving breakfast all day. The open-air design is perfect for the lakeside; you expect to see Bogart and Bacall lounging under the fan. Summers (across from the Palm) and the Beechtree Café (2066) are also popular with locals. The Beaches means ice cream, and everyone recommends Lick's at 1960 Queen East.

Time now to board the red rocket westbound for a trip to a village very different from the Beaches. Queen West came alive during the 1980s, with pawn shops and greasy spoons making room for anything young and funky. Everyone here strives to be new and different (you have seen the future and it has a pierced navel). The atmosphere is punk, androgenous, and distinctly child-free. A dose of brash capitalism is provided by numerous youthful street vendors.

Disembark at Spadina and walk east. The fashion scene is terrific, with a combination of new clothes from young designers and an exciting bunch of vintage clothing shops. Ms. Emma (275 Queen), Black Magic Vintage Clothing (323-A), and Marilyn Brooks (383) are shops not to miss. Skin and Bones (the eastern anchor to the street at 180) is Toronto's choice for mocassins, sheepskins and leathers.

The food on Queen West is diverse, to say the least. Judge for yourself by visiting the Parrot (325 Queen, nouvelle cuisine), Peter Pan

Strolling the boardwalk

(373, hangout for the youngish), the Queen Mother (everyone's favourite veggie menu) or the popular Avocado Club (165 John, light-hearted nouvelle).

Queen West considers itself to be a place of ideas, and appropriately the book shopping is par excellence, especially in the Queen and John vicinity. The Dragon Lady (comics, 200 Queen) and Bakka and Silver Snail (282 and 367, both sci-fi) have been favourites of Torontonians for years. About Books (280) and Pages (256) are heaven for the true bibliophile, with rare oldies of every description. The Can Do Book Store (311) sells guides to every skill you'll ever need. Edwards Books and Art (356) is near Spadina. Edwards is the only thing the Beaches and Queen West have in common.

Queen West is the place to catch Toronto's new music. Steve's Music Shop (415 Queen) is well known for selling anything that makes a sound, especially guitars. Popular music clubs are the Bam Boo (312) and the Rivoli (332); both have good food as well as music. The Horseshoe Tavern (370) is a holdover from Queen's seedier days and is still a landmark. By staying late on Queen West you can not only catch some up-and-coming musical acts, but the street begins to really come alive after dark. Sit tight on a restaurant patio and watch the night people.

This tale of one city has turned into a tale of two radically different neighbourhoods. Whether you prefer to wind up on Queen West or wind down at the Beaches, you're only a streetcar ride away.

Many stores and restaurants open Sunday

23

TORONTO/EAST YORK
Stars of the East

Hidden away in the east end of Toronto are two attractions that combine to make an unusual daytrip with a historic bent. Because the Riverdale Farm and the Todmorden Mills Museum are often overlooked by guidebooks, many Torontonians are surprised to find that only a mile or two away from downtown one can awaken to a rooster's crow or wander through an eighteenth-century settlement.

Begin the day at the Riverdale Farm, at the eastern extremity of Cabbagetown (itself an area worth a daytrip). Parking in the vicinity is at a premium; if you insist on driving, be prepared to park a few blocks away. Otherwise, walk south from the Castle Frank station

(Bloor-Danforth line) or take the Carlton streetcar eastbound from Yonge and then walk north along Sumach.

The Riverdale Farm is part of one of Toronto's earliest city parks, and visitors once travelled by street railway to tour the small zoo here. The zoo closed in the 1970s and the park was transformed into a nineteenth-century farm, complete with barns (relocated from Markham) and reproduction farmstead. It'll tickle your fancy to watch longhorn cattle munch away against a backdrop of fashionably renovated town homes. The Riverdale Farm runs popular programs for city kids, providing an opportunity to find out where eggs come from or to cuddle a fleecy lamb.

Todmorden Mills

The large animals are usually in outdoor paddocks, while the barns are home to chickens (very fresh eggs for sale daily), pigs, goats and sheep. Everyone loves to ooh and aah over newborns taking their first steps in the deep straw of the comfortable stalls. There are displays on egg production, breeds of farm animals, nutritious goat's milk and other pertinent information.

Pathways lead down into the valley of the Don River and Riverdale Park, which offers playing fields, a small wildlife sanctuary, wading pool and some good tobogganing. A good idea for lunch today is to have a picnic here. Bring your own supplies or buy them from the shops in Cabbagetown—there's one on almost every corner. The best known is More Than Cabbages (Carlton and Sackville), which will outfit you with a gourmet hamper.

Another restful stroll is through the Toronto Necropolis. It's just north of the farm and is the final resting place of many early Torontonians of note, such as William Lyon Mackenzie, George Brown, John Ross Robertson and Ned Hanlan. The Gothic Revival chapel and entrance to the Necropolis are considered the best example of the style in Canada, with a coloured slate roof, decorated bargeboards and gables.

Now we've enjoyed life on the farm nineteenth-century style, it's time to move on to the earliest settlement in the area, Todmorden Mills. Drive or walk to Bloor (Danforth) and take the subway or drive east to Broadview. Head north a few blocks to Pottery Road and travel down into the valley to find the Todmorden Mills Heritage Museum and Arts Centre.

This is a very old site by Toronto standards. Way back in 1794 grist and sawmills began operation, and later a paper mill, the second in Upper Canada, located here. Todmorden became a thriving business community when Thomas Helliwell opened a brewery around 1823; such enterprises thrived in York, with its large population of thirsty soldiers.

It's remarkable that so much of the settlement remains. The museum comprises two homes, the Helliwell brewery building, the Eastwood-Skinner paper mill and the 1881 Don railway station. The frame Regency cottage (the Terry house) was built on the site in 1797,

although most of the house dates to the 1820s and is furnished to the 1837 period. The spring which supplied the original settlers with water is still running, and the house was in continual occupancy until the 1960s.

The Helliwell house dates to the mid-1800s and is one of the few remaining mud-brick houses in Ontario. Costumed guides provide tours, pointing out the luxuries a wealthy mill owner of 1867 might enjoy, such as a wood stove (as opposed to an open hearth), wallpaper, sewing machine and piano. Helliwell kept extensive diaries of daily life at home and at the brewery, and museum staff incorporate these vivid descriptions in their tours. Both houses are the centre of special-event days, the most important of which is Simcoe Day (the August long weekend) when Mrs. Simcoe, brass bands, and a host of dignitaries turn out for games, food and fun.

The Helliwell brewery building contains exhibits on local history and geography, and also features a small gift shop. The Eastwood-Skinner Paper Mill, its brick smokestack a local landmark, was built in 1795 and is the oldest building in continuous use in the city. The mill has not been fancified like so many other historic industrial buildings—it remains the weathered red-brick workplace it started out as almost 200 years ago. The mill is now used by the Don Valley Art Club for art shows and summer school, and by the East Side Players for their popular summer theatre performances.

From watching speckled hens do pest-control duty along a city boulevard to learning how to make candles while the traffic on the Don Valley Expressway roars by, life in east-end Toronto turns up one beautiful surprise after another.

Riverdale Farm
Daily 9:00-dusk
(416) 392-7291

Todmorden Mills
May-January:
Tuesday to Friday 10:00-5:00
Saturday, Sunday and
Holidays 12:00-5:00
(416) 425-2250

24

EAST TORONTO
Sweet Surrender

Christmas shortbreads, birthday cake and ice cream, chocolate Easter eggs, Hallowe'en candies. If you're the kind of person whose calendar is a celebration of sweet treats, then Toronto is your kind of city. Toronto is home to a museum devoted to the world's favourite ingredient—sugar. Follow that appetizer with a tour of bakeries and confectioneries, shopping for sweet delicacies from around the world.

The Redpath Sugar Museum is located on Queen's Quay between Jarvis and Yonge, at the base of the Redpath silos that are familiar elements on the Toronto waterfront. Check in with the guard and head for the museum in the red-brick building facing the water. (As a sweetener, the museum throws in free parking.)

High-quality displays of maps, artifacts, historic photos and text trace the history of sugar use and production from hundreds of years B.C. to the present day. At one time an expensive luxury (in early England, one pound of sugar cost the same as 360 eggs), sugar became an inexpensive staple by 1800 due to the colonization of the Caribbean and to slavery. The museum devotes considerable space to the intertwined history of sugar and the "curse and crime" of African slavery, since low production costs resulted from low labour costs (fully two-thirds of African slaves were destined for sugar plantations). But sugar did not become the popular product it is today until the use of tea, coffee and chocolate became fashionable during the seventeenth and eighteenth centuries.

The museum also delves into the activities of Canada's sugar kings, especially John Redpath. A Montreal contractor, he built the first successful Canadian sugar-processing plant in 1854. A century later, Redpath Sugar became the first company to relocate to Toronto as a result of the St. Lawrence Seaway. Today, Redpath Sugar produces 1,000 tonnes of refined sugar daily (the plant operates 24 hours a day). The raw sugar comes from around the world by ship to Toronto.

There is probably no more universal ingredient than sugar. Be a sweet-tooth ambassador and take a tour of some of Toronto's international sweet shops. The tour starts near Danforth Avenue and Pape Avenue. Travel the easy way and take the Bloor-Danforth subway to Pape. If you insist on using private wheels, be warned that the parking in this part of town is horrendous, so leave the car in one spot and walk.

Run eagerly to the Pallas Bakery at 629 Danforth, in the heart of Toronto's "Little Athens." Naturally, you can count on wizardry with flaky filo dough, called tyropite if filled with feta cheese and baklava if filled with sweet and sticky ground nuts and honey. But you may not have counted on award-winning cake decorations, ouzo candies, tsoureki (egg bread), checkerboard cake, and profiteroles.

Stride briskly east on the Danforth (or take the subway to Greenwood) to number 1156, Burke's Bakery. Customers come from great distances to savour a wee bit o' the highlands. Here are all the solid and dependable Scots offerings: scones (potato, soda, raisin, and milk), buns (bap, oatmeal, whole wheat), shortbreads (in a variety of forms) and, of course, oatmeal cookies and gingerbread. The jelly doughnuts are extraordinarily good, as are the sausage rolls, meat pies and Christmas plum puddings.

Walk south on Greenwood to Gerrard, which has more sweet shops than any other thoroughfare in the city, and then east to Clayton's Candy. Don't let the humble exterior fool you, Reta Clayton's claim to the title of Queen of Canadian candymakers is undisputed. Since 1917, this shop has been producing mouth-watering horehound, humbug, peanut brittle, butterscotch drops, Turkish delight and licorice candies. If those names bring back fond memories, just wait till you see the antique scales and tiny brown bags. A rich piece of childhood hiding out on Gerrard Street.

Redpath Sugar Museum

Amble further east on Gerrard (don't groan about the walking, be grateful for the excuse for more heavy snacking). Milan's Department Store, the largest East Indian department store in North America, is at 1417 Gerrard. Indian sweets are Elysian concoctions of dairy products, sugar and honey. The staples at an Indian sweet shop are burfi (fudge offered in a rainbow of colours and flavours, like coconut and pistachio) and paan (sweet and savoury combinations eaten after a spicy meal to relieve the palate). Also try carrot halwah (carrots and condensed milk) and gulab jamun (round doughnuts in syrup).

Waddle westward on Gerrard to Pape. Just north of the intersection is the last stop of the day, Nicole's Truffles. If Clayton's represents the candy of the past, then Nicole's is the candy of the future. This delightful shop is pure comfort with its multi-pane windows outside and gleaming wood and carefully arranged flowers inside. Truffles come filled

with cappuccino, black raspberry, coconut cream, mandarin napoleon, and amaretto, and must compete with chocolate-covered ginger, orange peel and espresso beans. Every piece is handled slowly, with tender loving care, which serves to heighten the anticipation. Don't worry, the wait is well, well worth it.

Take a day to sample the offerings of some of the country's best bakers and confectioners, appreciating the way one simple ingredient can be transformed into a profusion of treats. Toronto: how sweet it is!

Redpath Sugar Museum
Monday-Friday 10:00-12:00
and 1:00-3:00
(416) 366-3561

Most bakeries closed Sunday

25

SCARBOROUGH/EAST TORONTO
Water, Water Everywhere

When Toronto old-timers recall the city of their youth, it doesn't take long for the talk to turn to glorious summers spent on the beaches along Lake Ontario. Today, the beaches in the city's east end remain popular daytrip destinations and the area has been joined by two modern-day attractions, the Leslie Street Spit, a mecca for bird-watchers and sailors, and the R.C. Harris Filtration Plant, an Art Deco fortress just waiting to be investigated.

Begin the day at the Leslie Street Spit (alias the Aquatic Park and Tommy Thompson Park). Travel west on Lakeshore Road and south on Leslie Street. The spit is a 5-kilometre pile of construction rubble and soil that was originally intended to be a breakwater for Toronto harbour. It is hard to believe that in only a few years the rubble has been transformed from lifeless eyesore to a parkland designated as environmentally significant, a haunt of naturalists, joggers, boaters and gardeners.

Mother Nature did most of the work, transporting seeds of trees and wildflowers from the mainland to the spit, where they quickly established themselves. The spit is an excellent place to appreciate first-hand the process called succession, the way in which mature plant communities replace the hardy pioneer plants which first colonize new territory. On the spit, small thickets of willow, Manitoba maple and cottonwood are taking over from Queen Anne's lace, goldenrod and milkweed.

The spit's claim to fame is its birds. It has one of two Caspian tern colonies on Lake Ontario. It is also home to more than 100,000 raucous ring-billed gulls, who appreciate living so close to the city's garbage-can smorgasbord. During spring and fall migration, hundreds of wading birds and sandpipers poke around in shallow ponds right under the noses of keen bird-watchers.

No cars are allowed on the Spit. TTC buses leave the entrance every hour or so from June to September and carry passengers to the lighthouse at the far end. The road is distance-posted for runners and walkers (no dogs allowed). The roadway is an excellent walk. On the one side, Lake Ontario provides an endless blue view, the waves crashing against rocks just below your feet. On the other side of the road, a sailboat harbour in a quiet lagoon is nearly hidden by tall cottonwood trees. On a still day this backwater is a mirror for masts and sails, a playground for families of geese and ducks, and a wonderful place for thoughtful reflection.

Now it's time to visit the beach. Drive north to Queen Street and head east to the Kew Gardens area a few blocks east of Woodbine. This neighbourhood has desperately few parking spots; try the public lot on Lee Avenue near the library. Walk south to the lakeshore and the Beaches boardwalk, a summertime gathering place for generations and a good place to use up some energy. You can sail, sailboard, swim (the water quality varies), fish and go boating. Or simply bask in the sun, enjoy the view and people-watch. The 2-kilometre boardwalk takes you to Woodbine Beach, an Olympic-sized pool, the Ashbridges Bay Yacht Club and public launch facilities, and a board-sailing school and rental facility.

Fresh air invigorates the appetite, and Queen Street has lots of restaurants and ice-cream stands to choose from. Or you can brown bag it in pleasant Kew Gardens.

Beaches and bird refuges are not all this stretch of shoreline has to offer. A worthwhile visit can be made to the R.C. Harris Filtration Plant, where lake water is turned into tap water. Walk or drive further east along Queen (turn right for parking along Nursewood Avenue). Visitors are sure to be impressed with the vast grounds of the plant. When the boardwalk becomes crowded on sultry afternoons, head for this parkland for sunbathing solitude and a wide-angle view of Scarborough Bluffs.

R.C. Harris Filtration Plant

The R.C. Harris plant is hailed as an outstanding example of Art Deco architecture, constructed in 1937, a time when utilitarian public buildings were designed to be community landmarks. The formidable yellow-brick exterior conceals interior views of surprising beauty, and the public is welcome in to view the plant on tours offered Saturdays and Sundays.

The tour highlight is the filter gallery, where huge pools of water slowly percolate through layers of sand, gravel and coal. The vast hallways are finished in acres of delicate marble, while the side galleries are cool, damp grottoes. The filtration plant is decorated at centre court by a marble and brass Edwardian clock standing a couple of metres high. The result is a rather mysterious beauty. It's also a little scary—the intense silence is broken only by the rhythmic drip of water. No wonder this place has been the backdrop for several television dramas.

The lakeside fun of old Toronto is still only a streetcar ride away. And better yet, the beach trip of today can include an urban wilderness and a remarkable marble fortress.

Tommy Thompson Park
June to Labour Day:
Saturday & Sunday 9:00-6:00
(416) 661-6600

R.C. Harris Filtration Plant (tours)
Saturday and Sunday
10:00, 11:30, 1:30 and 3:00
call ahead to check schedule

(416) 392-2932

26

SCARBOROUGH
A Natural Beauty

Scarborough doesn't get much good press these days—media wisecrackers nicknaming the city Scarberia because it is seen as a wasteland of car dealerships, strip shopping and most anything else that's tacky. But you can't believe everything you hear. A day spent in Scarborough takes in some great natural beauty spots, starting with the famous waterfront bluffs and ending with the magnificent Highland Creek valley.

Reach the bluffs by car or TTC along Kingston Road to Brimley Road. Head south, descending the 90-metre swoop of the road; if you end up in the lake, you've gone too far. Bluffer's Park is a sliver of parkland and marinas held between looming beige cliffs on one side and immense Lake Ontario on the other. It has become one of the city's precious spaces, enlivened by picnicking families, model boat and kite enthusiasts, boaters and sailors. Naturalists come to Bluffer's Park to study the bluff face, which is like an open book of Toronto's geological past. There are at least 10 layers of deposits that make up the bluffs, although only a few of these can be readily distinguished by the untrained observer. It's easiest to look for the telltale sign of water seepage which marks where a layer of sand sits overtop a layer of impermeable clay. The top layer of sediment is about 13,000 years old, while the lowest layer was laid down about 90,000 years ago.

Scarborough Bluffs

A trail follows the top of the bluffs. It can be reached by walking up Brimley Road to where the path crosses the roadway. Less athletic daytrippers may prefer to drive back to Kingston Road, west to Midland Avenue, then immediately left onto Scarboro Crescent. Follow Scarboro south to Drake Crescent; park along Drake and start walking in the quiet parkland/playground area along the top of the bluffs. The strange pointed formations known as Needles Bluffs give the area a western look and are Mother Nature's version of sculpture. The scenery is most dramatic in the fall, when the sumac covering the cliffs turns crimson and the fields atop the bluffs are bright with blooming aster and goldenrod.

Another site for studying Lake Ontario in her summer blues or winter greys is the Guild Inn. Drive east on Kingston Road and follow the Guildwood Parkway a couple of kilometres to the inn. The Guild Inn has an interesting history. In 1932 this country estate was purchased by Spencer and Rosa Clark, who opened their home for use as studios and shops for weavers, sculptors and painters, hoping to provide artists relief from the Depression. The arts flourished here, and accommodation and dining were added to the estate. For the daytripper, the Guild Inn offers satisfying meals (fabulous weekend brunches) in a room with a sweeping view of the gardens and lake (reservations suggested). The Guild continues to support the arts, and the gift shop sells the work of many talented painters, sculptors and artisans.

The Clarks expanded their charitable work to include salvaging portions of fine old downtown buildings that were being demolished to make way for modern development. Some 60 architectural relics—huge columns, entire entranceways, decorative panels, urns and gargoyles—now reside in the lovely woods and gardens surrounding the Guild, making it an unconventional park indeed. The most famous of the buildings represented include the Bank of Montreal from King and Bay streets (1948), the Granite Club (1926), the Bank of Toronto from King and Bay (1912), and the Bank of Nova Scotia building, 39 King West (1903).

From man-made beauty, it's back to the beauty of nature. Drive east on Guildwood Parkway to Morningside Avenue and then north. Drive slowly over Highland Creek to savour the view of the valley forest—in the fall the colours are without equal anywhere in Toronto. To explore the valley further, drive into Scarborough College, the eastern branch of the University of Toronto. Pathways begin from behind the large campus building which snakes along the rim of the valley.

The pathways travel through mature deciduous and coniferous forest that is largely undisturbed on the valley slopes, although the valley floor and riverbanks have been reduced to meadow or parkland. Look for some of Toronto's largest hemlock and white pine, both of which are sensitive to the effects of air pollution and are not usually found in such densely populated areas. The forest also contains maple, oak, beech and cedar. The walkways along Highland Creek continue south for as long as you want to walk. If it's a day for a family picnic, Morningside Park on the west side of Morningside Avenue has plenty of playing fields and picnic grounds, along with more fine valley hiking.

One purpose of travel is to dispel stereotypes. A trip to Scarborough will have us changing our tune from Scarberia to Scarborough, a natural beauty.

Guild Inn, Oak Dining Room
(416) 261-3331

CAMPBELLVILLE
On the Rocks

OK, you may have driven past the Niagara Escarpment a thousand times, the looming grey cliffs a familiar sight to travellers on the 401, but have you ever appreciated the uniqueness of this landform? Dozens of rare plants and animals call the escarpment home; an Indian settlement thrived here long before white exploration; and where else in southern Ontario can you climb cliffs and experience such sensational views? Discover the escarpment's natural charms by visiting three varied conservation areas near Campbellville.

Crawford Lake Conservation Area, the centre-piece of Halton's escarpment parks, is just east of Guelph Line on Steeles Avenue, 3 kilometres south of the 401. Head for the nature centre for an introduction to life on the escarpment. Displays, slide shows, special events and a children's discovery room focus on the area's unique combination of geological, botanical and zoological features. Some of Crawford Lake's special residents include a carnivorous plant called the sundew, over 40 varieties of fern, and nesting turkey vultures. Park naturalists conduct frequently scheduled walks on 13 kilometres of hiking and groomed ski trails. Crawford Lake is unique in having specially designed "wilderness" wheelchairs for rent.

Crawford Lake Conservation Area has two highlights. One is the boardwalk around tiny and fragile Crawford Lake. This spot has a very northern feel to it, shaded and cool all summer with numerous rocky outcrops. The special nature of the lake—meromictic, meaning minimal water circulation—means that the sediment in the bottom has been undisturbed for thousands of years. Sediment tests led scientists to search for, and find, relics of an Iroquois village, once home to hundreds of people. This is the first Eastern Woodland Indian site preserved in such detail. A tour of the reconstructed village is the second highlight of Crawford Lake. Explanatory notes guide visitors through longhouses complete with sleeping platforms and artifacts, palisades and Indian gardens. Learn about native hunting, fishing, tobacco-growing, games, festivals and burial rites. There is a full schedule of special events based on the Indian calendar.

Armed with a greater understanding of the escarpment environment, drive on to Mount Nemo Conservation Area. Take Guelph Line south. Guelph Line is a great country drive any time of the year, hilly and winding, with new scenery at every turn. It is especially good in the fall, when crimson and gold leaves contrast with the green lawns surrounding rustic retreats. Find picnic supplies at the pretty Lowville General Store (the ice cream is especially recommended). Mount Nemo is about 7 kilometres south of Crawford Lake. There is a small sign at the junction of Guelph Line and Colling Road. Park on the shoulder of the road; the 1 1/2-kilometre hiking trail begins right here.

At first Mount Nemo seems typical of the Ontario countryside: pastureland and birch and maple woods, wildflowers in white, purple and gold. It is at the very end of the trail that something extraordinary occurs. You approach a stone lookout built at the very rim of the escarpment. The view beyond is concealed by the stone parapet. As you mount each step, a wider and grander vista is slowly revealed. Visitors gasp as they see the whole prospect: Toronto, the CN Tower and Lake Ontario in the distance, with neat farms and estate homes hundreds of feet below. Well worth the walk.

It's time to move on to the last visit of the day, Rattlesnake Point Conservation Area. Just getting there is part of the fun. Head north on Guelph Line, east along Britannia Road to Appleby Line, and then north to Rattlesnake Point. You drive *up* the escarpment face, hairpin curves revealing brief, glorious views. (Drivers aren't allowed to take their eyes off the narrow road.)

Crawford Lake

Rattlesnake Point is over 200 hectares of cliff-top hiking and groomed skiing, with several lookout points at the very brink of the grey precipice. Although the trails are not long and are well worn, they are rugged enough that you can imagine yourself an explorer for a few hours. This location is frequently used by climbers, so if you are feeling full of yourself for today's lengthy perambulation, just stop and watch the effort these helmeted folk put into clawing their way up the elevation you just drove. Rattlesnake Point is a good for a picnic, with lots of tables, barbeque sites, washrooms and playing fields.

This tour of three conservation areas will heighten your appreciation for one of Ontario's most precious and unique scenic areas, the grand Niagara Escarpment. Take a day to explore life on the rocks.

Crawford Lake Conservation Area
Public programs
Saturday, Sunday & Holidays 10:00-4:00
(416) 854-0234 (site)
(416) 336-1158 (administration)

Mount Nemo Conservation Area
Daily, year-round

Rattlesnake Point Conservation Area
Daily 8:30-dusk
(416) 887-1147 (site)
(416) 335-1158 (administration)

28

OAKVILLE
Country Living in the City

At one point or another, the call of country living beckons us to consider whether we'd be more content if the kids had a hayloft to play in, if a trout stream rushed near our home, if woodland trails were only a moment away. Well, fantasize no more, for such a life is ours (if only for a day) when we visit Bronte Creek Provincial Park. Although Bronte Creek is within sight of the spreading fingers of the city, it offers the wide open spaces and varied outdoor activity that most people expect to travel hours to find. The park is located on the outskirts of Oakville; exit the QEW at Burloak Drive north and follow the road signs.

Bronte Creek's human history dates back almost 7,000 years, with native people occupying this area from 5000 B.C. until about 1820. Since that time the land has been used primarily for agriculture, and the Spruce Lane Farm is a reminder of this use. The farm is worked by horse and plow, demonstrating the methods and equipment used at the turn of this century. Visitors are welcome to pick fruit in the extensive apple and pear orchards in the fall. At the farmstead, urban kids can try their hand at domestic chores such as shearing, spinning and quilting.

A second farm area, the Children's Farm, has been developed as a play area, its petting zoo providing ponies, cattle, chickens and pigs to feed and fondle. An adventure playground par excellence is located in a large barn (just the ticket when it rains on family picnic day). It was pure inspiration that divided the barn according to age levels, the lower area for children up to five years and the lofts for children five to ten years, allowing each group to play rambunctiously yet safely. There are Tarzan ropes, catwalks, tunnels, swinging bridges and, of course, lots of equipment for general clambering about— heaven for kids (and for parents, who watch the fun just a little wistfully).

The Visitors' Centre near the Children's Farm contains changing displays on the natural and human history of the site. Don't miss the opportunity to scrutinize the private workings of a beehive. The centre has a glass hive with an entrance to the outdoors so that the comings and goings can be observed without causing anxiety for bees or humans.

The central portion of the park is devoted to outdoor exercise. Like the Children's Farm, this area has been planned to allow for many kinds of users. The vast outdoor pool teems with people of all ages. The water is shallow and warm, making it ideal for young waders, but the size allows real swimmers to have their fun, too. There are tennis, basketball and volleyball courts, two fitness trails and shuffleboard. The park concession rents all the appropriate equipment, from basketballs to barbecues.

During the winter, Bronte Creek provides one of the finest toboggan hills around—long, wide and fast. The large natural skating rink and the toboggan hill are floodlit for nighttime fun. The hiking trails of summer turn into cross-country ski trails during the winter; call ahead if you wish to rent skis, skates or snowshoes. And if you are visiting during December, there is usually hot cider and baked goods at Spruce Lane Farm.

For those who wish a little solitude with their fresh air, Bronte has two walking trails, each with an excellent interpretive booklet available from park staff. Mice, Men & Maiden's Blush is the moniker for a 1-kilometre trail near the visitors' centre. The trail booklet describes the process of natural regeneration as native forest begins to overtake farm fields abandoned in the 1960s. Features along the trail which remain from the days of agriculture, such as white pine stumps, orchards with uncommon Maiden's Blush apples, and spruce hedgerows, are noted in the trail guide.

The Half Moon Trail Valley (2 kilometres) winds up and down the naturally terraced river valley that was a Mississauga Indian

Children's Farm

reserve until 1820. The trail passes through stretches of beautiful upland forest of birch, maple and stately white pine. The forest colour is spectacular in fall, while in spring there are plenty of trilliums to photograph. The trail guide discusses the impact of such pioneer activities as brickmaking and mill construction on the natural environment. Pause at the lookout point high above Bronte Creek. You may see visitors fishing for trout and salmon in the stream. A scene reminiscent of pioneer days? No, for logging and agriculture destroyed the stream habitat for fish, and it is only due to modern development (resulting in the removal of mill dams and in local reforestation) that Bronte Creek again supports a small sport fishery.

The Ontario Ministry of Natural Resources calls Bronte Creek its first near-urban park, and due to clever planning it is an unqualified success, managing to offer a generous slice of country life to ordinary city folk. This is a place you'll keep coming back to.

Bronte Creek Provincial Park
Daily 8:00-dusk
Mid-December to March,
skating until 9:30 pm

Spruce Lane Farm
Sunday-Thursday 9:00-4:00
(hours vary during fall and winter)

Children's Farm
Daily 9:00-4:00

(416) 335-0023 (Burlington)
(416) 827-6911 (Oakville)

29

OAKVILLE
Drop Anchor in Oakville

Lake Ontario is one of the world's great inland seas. The lake shaped Ontario's development in countless ways, as every river mouth became an active harbour site, sending settlers to the frontier, and forest and farm products to Europe. Sadly, many early harbour towns in central Ontario lost their business to road and rail, and lost their soul to urban sprawl. We are fortunate in being able to visit Oakville, which retains much of its original charm even as it acts as a busy recreational port of today.

Start a day in old Oakville at the Oakville Museum (take Navy south off Lakeshore Road to the corner of Navy and Front streets). The museum is on the Erchless Estate, in buildings constructed from 1835 to 1934 and used as a home as well as a store, customs house and bank. The estate includes the charming Customs House and Toronto Bank building, which are shaded by tall trees and cooled by lake breezes. Eastward, Erchless faces Lakeside Park, the place to be on a summer's day, especially when a band concert is on. Westward, it has an eagle's-eye view of busy Oakville harbour on Sixteen Mile Creek.

Inside the museum, attractive information-packed displays of text, photos and artifacts describe the development of the port of Oakville under the headings of founding fathers, seasonal labourers, merchants, mariners and summer visitors. It is not surprising that Oakville was a shipbuilding town of renown, but few people realize that it was also a strawberry and basket town, and that as early as 1900 it was a holiday resort, attracting daytrippers from Toronto and Hamilton.

Continue your trip through time by stepping outside with the walking-tour brochure available at the museum. The rush of commuter life seems a distant dream as you stroll under tall trees, looking at some of the best-preserved and most elegant nineteenth-century homes in Ontario. Oakville's symmetrical frame Georgian homes provide a refreshing contrast to the brick Victoriana of the rest of Ontario. Plaques on the historic homes indicate the name and occupation of the original resident, a nice touch that makes history more personal.

Walk east along Front Street to Lakeside Park and the Old Post Office and Thomas House. Thomas House (1829) is a tiny log cabin moved to this site from a nearby farm. The Post Office, Oakville's first, houses changing displays that are especially geared to children, with lots of historical quizzes, games and hands-on fun.

Continue east on Front Street. As you pass Thomas Street, glance at the charming row of houses starting at number 18 (1852). These were built by shipmaster and merchant Duncan Chisholm (a nephew of town father William Chisholm) and have also been used as labourers' quarters. Across the street at number 29 Thomas stands Glenorchy (1839), home of Peter MacDougald, grain merchant and early mayor of Oakville.

The historic homes of Oakville are superbly crafted. This is because many were the homes of shipbuilders: if you could manage to turn Ontario oak into a vessel capable of weathering November gales, you could build a solid home. One example is 176 Front Street, one of Oakville's best Georgian homes. Another landmark is the Worn Doorstep (1870) at 212 Front Street. Originally a residence for the groom of William Chisholm, this was a tearoom for daytrippers until the 1940s, when it again became a private home.

Turn away from the lake on Dunn Street. Leather manufacturer and famed yachtsman Cecil Marlatt built the estate at 43 Dunn (1888), the only brick home on the tour, and one which includes all the architectural embellishments of the times: turrets, gingerbreading, dormers and bay windows. Walk east along King or William Street to Reynolds Street and Oakville's oldest place of worship,

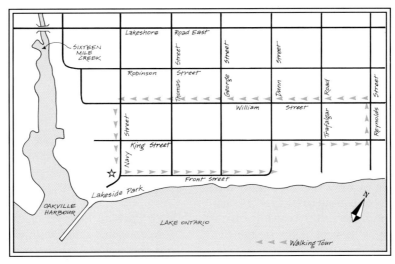

Oakville

St. Andrew's Church, largely unchanged from how it appeared in 1840. Not all churches fare so well. Walk west on William Street to the Scotch Kirk at numbers 296-301. Built in 1850, this building was originally a Presbyterian church, and it had a stern and sober look that reflected the reputation of its parishioners.

Number 308 William is an enchanting Regency cottage built in the 1850s. The low-pitched hip roof, decorated doorway and picket fence combine to create a picture-perfect little house. Continue west along William, stopping to admire St. Jude's Church (1883) with its stained-glass window commemorating Queen Victoria's jubilee. Take a pleasant detour through the gardens on the west side of the church. Number 148 William is the residence of the sexton. This Gothic Revival house, with its steep gables, rounded windows and shutters, is a contrast to most of the other homes in historic Oakville.

Spend some time exploring other streets in old Oakville. If you visit during the summer, be sure to conclude the tour on Navy Street near the lawn-bowling club. Although it is hard to sort the players from the spectators—everyone being dressed in whites—there's no doubt that this is one of Oakville's cherished spots. When evening shadows creep over Navy Street and the clink of the bowls is the only sound around, it seems like this scene has been played out for countless summers.

When in a harbour town, dine on fish. It is a short drive to Sharkey's on the Water (111 Forsythe Street, west along Lakeshore and then north immediately after the bridge). From squid to swordfish, seafood is the star at Sharkey's. There is a wonderful terraced patio overlooking Sixteen Mile Creek and the action in the upper harbour. Sunday brunch is lavish, with salads, eggs Benedict and shellfish, including steamed mussels. To keep you in the waterfront frame of mind, from April to October Canadian Fishing Adventures operates fishing charters and pleasure cruises from Sharkeys. There's more seafood at popular Shelley's, located on the east side of Sixteen Mile Creek just north of the museum (closed Sunday).

What to do in a port town? Do some boat-watching, of course. So after a meal, head to the mouth of Sixteen Mile Creek, and Oakville's busy port. Boat-watching is a spectator sport here, with visitors sitting on deck chairs near the breakwater, observing the constant manoeuvrings of yachts, dinghies, sailboats, speedboats and fishing boats. It's a good way to get a sailor's tan without mortgaging the house to buy your own boat.

Oakville Museum
Tuesday-Friday 1:00-5:00
Saturday, Sunday & Holidays 12:00-5:00
(416) 845-3952

Thomas House & Post Office
May-September:
Sunday-Friday 12:00-5:00
(416) 845-3952

30

MILTON
Down on the Farm

Urbanites live in a landscape that is in a constant state of flux. Familiar landmarks are remodelled or disappear and lifestyles adjust to fit a parade of new technologies. We also live with the notion that rural Ontario is stable and unchanging, patiently waiting on the urban fringe for us to visit. This image of country life may be comforting but it is erroneous, as a daytrip to Milton can reveal.

Visit the 32-hectare Ontario Agricultural Museum, which chronicles the ongoing evolution of rural life. Exit the 401 north at Milton and drive west on Regional Road 9 to Tremaine Road and then south to the museum. Learn how life on the farm, from machinery to marketing, is always changing, and how these changes are reflected in landscapes, settlement patterns and commerce throughout Ontario.

Three farmsteads (one under development), complete with outbuildings and livestock, form the nucleus of the museum. They represent three generations of farming—the 1830s, the 1860s and the 1890s. The 1890s farm includes the octagonal Troyer-Fraser barn, a landmark to travellers on the 401.

Costumed guides demonstrate routine tasks such as candle-making and soap-making; children are accorded a special welcome and

Ontario Agricultural Museum

helping hand. These activities illustrate how very different life has been for each successive farm generation as drudgery diminishes and creature comforts multiply. Reminders that farm life includes much more than feeding livestock and growing grain are found in displays on skills such as shingle-making, well-drilling and fur-ranching. The spacious grounds of the museum also feature one of the largest collections of farm machinery and implements on the continent, from tractors to corn pickers.

The most unique feature of this museum is the Crossroads Community, which is a snapshot of small-town Ontario caught between the pioneer age and the present day. Displays of historic tools, photographs and explanatory material are arranged in a collection of buildings from church to gas station.

Templin's Carriage Works, relocated from Fergus to the Crossroads, illustrates the evolution of farm support industries from the late 1800s to the present day. Technical know-how and business resiliency allowed an eighteenth-century blacksmith and carriage-maker to prosper over decades of rapid technological and social change. As the farm community surrounding Fergus expanded and prospered, there was increased demand for specialized farm products. Templin diversified to include the manufacture of fanning mills (which separate grain from chaff). One might predict that the transformation of Ontario from a horse-driven to a gasoline-driven society would see Templin's go out of business, but it adapted once again by becoming Templin's Garage, which it remained until after World War II.

The Crossroads Community includes a Women's Auxiliary Hall. Find out about the four-million-member worldwide rural educational and service organization that began in Stoney Creek, Ontario. A study of the Auxiliary is a testament to the evolving role of women in agriculture, as the focus of attention moves from home-making skills (instruction on sewing machines) to consumer advocacy (the Women's Auxiliary was instrumental in the fight for milk pasteurization and rural highway speed limits, among many things).

To complete your journey through the countryside, visit Chudleigh's Farm, just north of the Agricultural Museum on Highway 25. Chudleigh's provides an opportunity to see a modern-day farm in action and to enjoy some of its harvest. At Chudleigh's the popular pick-you-own form of marketing is combined with a farmyard-turned-amusement-park to give everyone in the family something to do.

Chudleigh's orchards are planted with several varieties of apples, so that there is fresh picking from mid-August until November. Varieties include MacIntosh and Delicious and a number of lesser known but equally appealing types such as Tydeman and Wealthy. The suitability of each variety for eating, cooking and sauce-making is noted on a chalkboard in the entrance area. There is also cider for fridge or freezer, produced daily on the premises and available at bargain-basement prices. The cost of pick-your-own apples depends on the quantity picked and the day of the week (midweek being least expensive), so bring a host of enthusiastic helpers and a wagon for ease in transporting your haul. Less energetic participants ride a large tractor-pulled wagon to the orchards.

And Chudleigh's is not just apples, as corn and pumpkins are available in season. In winter, hot cider awaits skiers enjoying the cross-country trails. Weekends are especially active at Chudleigh's, with pony and trail rides for children and outdoor food stands which sell natural food snacks and light meals. The adventure playground with a hayloft theme teems with noisy kids.

In one day we have travelled from an isolated farmstead of the 1830s to the excitement of Chudleigh's during apple harvest. There may be no more enjoyable way to appreciate the transformation of rural Ontario over 160 years.

Ontario Agricultural Museum
Mid-May to mid-September:
Daily 10:00-5:00
(416) 878-8151

Chudleigh's
November-August:
Wednesday-Sunday 10:00-5:00
August-November:
Daily 9:00-7:00
(416) 270-2982 (Toronto)
(416) 878-2725 (Milton)

31

GEORGETOWN
Rural Roots

Suburbanization and the commuter syndrome has struck Ontario in a big way, stripping many rural villages of their unique character and overshadowing their original raison d'être. But every once in a while we can discover a place that has not turned its back on its economic roots, a place that "sticks to the knitting," continuing the work of past generations. Three such towns—Georgetown, Acton and Erin—are located conveniently close together, allowing for an interesting daytrip.

Travel west on Highway 7 towards Georgetown, or take the 401 and exit north on Trafalgar Road. Georgetown started out as a farm-and-mill community during the mid-1880s. Economic prosperity brought the railway. The combination of good growing conditions and rapid transportation to large markets meant Georgetown was a prime location for the horticultural trade. As one example, the Dominion Seed House has been in business here since the 1920s. It is on Highway 7 just east of town, where Highway 7 and Maple Avenue intersect.

Visit during the growing season and you can't miss Dominion Seed: the garden centre is enveloped by fields that are a tapestry of flowers in hues from delicate to dynamic. The fields are used not only to supply fresh flowers and potted plants for the nursery, but also to produce seed. The centre is a great find for green thumbs, with plants, seed (flower, vegetable and even tree varieties impossible to obtain elsewhere), soil mixes and books. There's also a good selection of bird houses and feeders, and for the small sprouts there's a children's corner. Advice on gardening and landscaping is first-rate.

Drive west through town on Highway 7 and head for Acton. Even though Acton is only a short drive from Georgetown, its history and character is very different. Acton is best known as "Leathertown," a tanning centre since 1842. Leather is still the largest employer in town. In the mid-1800s the Beardmore

Tanning Company proclaimed itself the largest tannery in the British Empire. One of the Beardmore warehouses is now the Olde Hide House (located on Eastern Avenue just south of Highway 7).

If you don't like spending money, brace yourself, it's hard to resist the incredible selection of leather clothing at the Olde Hide House. There is a full line of men's and women's coats, suits, pants, gloves and wallets. If you can imagine it in leather, it is here waiting for you in a dozen colours. But the Olde Hide House is much more than just leather. Some daytrippers come simply to eat at Jack Tanner's Table: good food in an unusual setting. The menu features beef (what would you expect of an honest tannery?), but also offers seafood and pasta. Servings are generous and prices good (open daily).

Acton has two more shops that remind us of its tanning heritage. On Mill Street, the main drag, there's Flight-Line. If you fantasize about being a flying ace, Flight-Line will outfit you from their full range of aviation leathers. On Church Street near Highway 25, Warehouse West is made for Roy and Dale, with cowboy gear from boots to chaps to 10-gallon hats. Bid happy trails to Acton and gallop along Highway 25 north to Ospringe and then east along Highway 24 to Erin.

Erin is another town that began as a mill site, Daniel McMillan harnessing the Credit River for lumber, grist and oat mills during the 1860s. Of the three towns visited today, Erin retains the closest ties with its nineteenth-century roots. The mill located on Main Street, Mundell Lumber Company, is Ontario's last remaining planing mill still operated by water power (it has the capacity to run on conventional electricity as well).

There are other glimpses of a mill town that grew into a rural service centre. In operation since 1943, Steen's Dairy is one of the province's last independent dairies. What a rare treat it is

Erin Fall Fair, Thanksgiving weekend

to sit at the counter and observe the unhurried comings and goings of Erin: the grocer coming in for coffee, price gun tucked in his belt; truckers stopping for "home burgers"; farm families enjoying a cone during their day in town. Steen's makes some of the best chocolate ice cream you'll ever taste—good thing there's a dairy case full for take-out.

With a planing mill on the main drag, no wonder Erin is a terrific wood-floor town, many of the Main Street shops displaying well-worn beauties. Houlton's Bakery (closed Sundays) is one such shop, but the floors aren't any competition for the cookies, muffins, pies and cakes. The prices at both Steen's and Houlton's will have you wondering if Erin has entered the twentieth century at all. More comfy floors welcome you at the Boston Mills Press, which offers a handsome stable of books on Ontario's natural beauty and history (closed Sundays). Check out the sale table near the front door.

It sometimes takes a little searching to find Ontario's rural roots. Georgetown, Acton and Erin make the search enjoyable, as they successfully incorporate elements of their early history with their contemporary character.

Dominion Seed House
Monday-Friday 9:00-6:00
Saturday 9:00-5:00
During spring and summer
Thursday & Friday 9:00-8:00
Sunday 12:00-4:00
(416) 877-2801

The Olde Hide House
(519) 853-1031

32

BELFOUNTAIN
A-Hunting We Will Go

The rivers that flow south into Lake Ontario—Rouge, Don, Humber, Credit and Bronte—are critical elements in the geography and history of the province. Indian trails along these rivers date back thousands of years, and the rivers were highways for European explorers and settlers. For generations daytrippers have rambled the Credit River Valley, enjoying the cool water and the fine fall foliage. Spend a memorable day antique-hunting along the scenic sideroads of the Credit Valley from Glen Williams to Alton, visiting quaint shops and perhaps locating that perfect piece of valley history to take home with you.

This daytrip twists and rolls through the river valley, so you may want to have a detailed map of the area with you before you set out, or perhaps purchase one at a store along the way. Begin the day at Glen Williams, located just northeast of Georgetown. To find the Glen, either drive north on Highway 10 and west on Old School Road, or from Georgetown, take Mountainview Road north (to confuse you, it's also known as 9th Line, Regional Road 13 and Confederation Street) to Main Street in Glen Williams.

Glen Williams may be the most appealing Credit Valley town. It's a wonder that it has stayed so tiny and unaffected despite its close proximity to Toronto. Glen Williams dates back to 1825, when the Williams family built water-powered lumber and grist mills in this spot. The original Williams sawmill still stands and the rushing stream can be heard throughout the village. There remain several fine homes that belonged to the original founding families.

The antique-hunter will want to head for Marie Beaumont Antiques in the attractive red-brick home on Main Street built by village merchant Charles Williams. Immaculately restored pine harvest tables, bureaus and chests from across eastern Canada are housed in the equally immaculate barn at the rear of the property.

While in Glen Williams, visit Clay Concepts Studio & Gallery. Carol-Ann Michaelson produces fine pottery in this shop where Timothy Eaton first clerked. A good snack can be had at the Copper Kettle Inn, which has a British pub feel to it, complete with competition dart sets.

Drive east on Old School Road and north on Winston Churchill Boulevard to find Terra Cotta, located on the Credit River flats. Although antiques are hard to find in Terra Cotta (unless you consider the nineteenth-century general store an antique), there's lots here of interest to the daytripper. The pretty and popular Terra Cotta Inn has been dispensing food to travellers for years, including afternoon teas and Sunday brunches. The Forge Studio has works of art in clay that are a welcome relief from the standard mug sets, as well as bright watercolours and blown-glass art. The Brass Thimble specializes in prints of local scenes and wildlife. Just north of Terra Cotta on Winston Churchill Boulevard is the Terra Cotta Conservation Area. There's lots here to keep visitors busy: camping, swimming, fishing (stocked trout ponds), orienteering, hiking on the Bruce Trail, mini-golfing and nature interpretation programs.

Time to return to the Credit River. Drive back to Terra Cotta and east along King Street (the main east-west street) to Chinguacousy Road. Turn north to find Boston Mills House antiques (between Boston Mills Road and Old Base Line Road). Boston Mills House, a mill house dating to 1864, is a treasure chest for antique lovers. Four rooms are filled to over-flowing with silver, china, brass and primitive housewares. The items span centuries, so if you're searching for a particular piece of Spode or Wedgwood to complete a prized set, or if you hanker after silver Edwardian decanter labels, don't miss the Boston Mills House (weekends only or by appointment).

Take Boston Mills Road or Old Base Line Road east to Highway 10 and then head

Belfountain

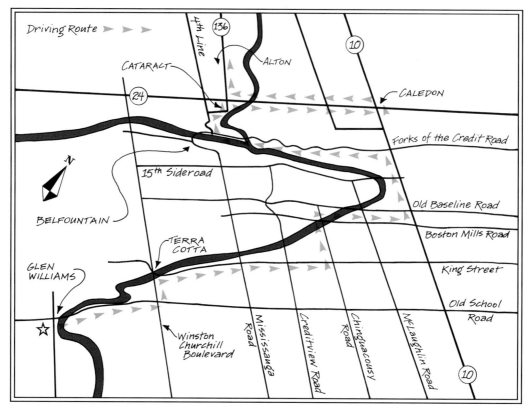

Belfountain

north. Victoria Antiques has a large collection of huge furniture—all those extra-long dining tables, towering wardrobes and massive bedroom suites that won't fit in most antique shops can be found here. The condition varies from deluxe to delapidated (cobwebs free of charge), which makes this a fun browse.

Continue north on Highway 10. (This portion of the tour takes you a little away from the Credit Valley proper but into prime antique country.) A few kilometres brings you to the Lamplighter Shoppe. The proverbial bull in a china shop wouldn't fare much better here, with shelf upon shelf of antique glass lamps. Some are charming workaday models from the nineteenth-century pioneer, others are more elaborate affairs with romantically decorated tall chimneys. All are meticulously labelled as to vintage and style.

Turn west off Highway 10 at Forks of the Credit Road, which leads to Belfountain through some of the prettiest scenery in southern Ontario. The trip through the river gorge named Forks of the Credit, just east of Belfountain, is so much fun you'll want to

drive it again. Where else near Toronto can you find so many switchbacks and hidden corners? The Forks was once a quarry town, the massive cliffs being carved into building stone for the grand buildings of Toronto, such as the Parliament Buildings and Old City Hall. But distance to Toronto (there was no road here, only the famous Credit Valley Railway) and difficult topography resulted in quarry abandonment and the valley reverted to nature. (A word to the wise: avoid the area on fall weekends, for although the leaf colour is sensational, auto fumes and crowded hiking trails make it a less than romantic getaway. Save your trip for weekdays or off-season.)

The town of Belfountain has a number of shops worth a visit. Credit Creek Country Store and Hawkes' Antiques are located in the centre of town. Plaid pigs, calico teddys and pewter jewellery share space with antique weather vanes, rocking horses, churns and cradles. Head for Tubtown Antiques if you want a conversation piece: ancient coffee mills, wooden shovels, candle boxes, box churns operated by a side crank, all superbly restored. Find an excellent display of antique hand tools at Belfountain Antiques, as well as decoys and horse brasses.

Drop in at the Belfountain General Store for something to snack on while hiking at the conservation area. Home baking includes country pecan bars, banana or rocky road squares, and brambleberry pie. Head down into the river valley to find the Belfountain Conservation Area. There's pleasant walking along the river, swimming (when water quality permits), fishing and picnicking. This is an ideal spot for stretching your legs and looking at the river.

Drive to the village of Caledon by travelling north along the 4th Line from Belfountain (following signs for a jog through pretty Cataract with its inn) and then head east along Highway 24. Caledon is a detour from the Credit Valley, taken for its remarkable shop, Clark House Antiques. This is actually three stores—Tall Stories, Carol Edwards Antiques and Mac's Tiques—in an old home with a quaint wooden front porch. The Clark House has elegant furniture that includes once-in-a-lifetime finds, such as an ebony tête-a-tête with mother-of-pearl inlay. Plus there are lots of mahogany stacking tables, butler's chests, writing tables, antique prints and fine porcelain. The Willow, around the corner from the Clark House, provides good contrast, with primitive Canadiana such as wool winders, mail boxes, wooden buckets and more.

Back to the Credit Valley and the village of Alton. Take Highway 24 west to Highway 136 north. Alton is another mill town. The Wright Brothers started flour milling here in the mid-1800s. The Dods Knitting Mill soon followed and made its fame by supplying WWI soldiers with socks. That mill has been refurbished as the Millcroft Inn, which is making a name for itself as the star attraction of the Credit Valley. Follow the directional signs through town.

Everyone should dine at the Millcroft (or better yet, spend a weekend). The main inn building dates to 1881 and is still perched at the brink of the cliffs overlooking Shaw's Creek, a tributary of the Credit. This elegant resort offers cross-country skiing, bicycling, skating and canoeing on the millpond, hiking (the Bruce Trail passes near here), a sauna and an outdoor pool. The interior retains the massive stone and polished beams of the mill, and the guest rooms are bountifully supplied with creature comforts like extra-large beds, ample duvets and antique furnishings.

The dining (lunch, dinner or afternoon tea) deserves its excellent reputation. The menu includes Caledon trout with lemon and pine nuts, venison pâté with Cumberland sauce, medallions of veal with orange-ginger sauce, and the Mill's own ice-cream pie with raspberry sauce. The dining room overlooks the waterfall, cedar forest and millpond; it seems even the fallen trees and wildflowers have been carefully orchestrated for effect. The canopied summer dining patio is much photographed. Dining at the Millcroft is simply the perfect end to the day.

Enjoy the thrill of the hunt: driving around a hairpin curve to find a village that looks the same as it has for 150 years; discovering that piece of crystal to complete Grandma's set; finally locating that perfect shade of milk paint for your next project. And there's no place more perfect for your hunt than the scenic Credit River Valley, located less than one hour from Toronto. Happy hunting.

Terra Cotta Inn
(416) 453-8261

Millcroft Inn
(519) 941-8111

Terra Cotta Conservation Area
January to Thanksgiving, daily
Thanksgiving to January,
Monday to Friday
(416) 877-9650 (site)
(416) 670-1615 (administration)

Belfountain Conservation Area
Mid-April to Thanksgiving:
Daily 8:00-7:00
(519) 927-5838 (site)
(416) 670-1615 (administration)

33

MONO CENTRE
Hikers, Bikers and the Hockley Valley

Ah, a Sunday afternoon free from chores! For generations Ontarians have headed to the hills and valleys of Peel and Dufferin counties northwest of Toronto for fresh air and country scenery. Despite suburbia's determined march toward the countryside, the Hockley Valley near Orangeville is still a great place to explore gravel sideroads and woodsy trails.

Highway 10 leads north past Orangeville. After a short drive north of town, head east along the Hockley Valley Road; it is well signposted. Leave your city driving habits behind, slow down, and enjoy the passing scenery. It seems as if time has forgotten the Hockley Valley Road, leaving it to loop through the valley or crisscross the river (a tributary of the Nottawasaga) over tiny bridges. You pass modest rural retreats built decades ago, now sitting cheek by jowl with modern country estates. The entire valley is good for leaf-watching during the fall, when scarlet and orange contrast with the cedar woods along the river and the plantations of pine on the hills.

If you long for the gravel roads of childhood memory, any of the sideroads in the Hockley Valley are worthwhile detours. Drive north on Mono Road 3. In a few short kilometres the route covers some steep driving, a narrow bridge over the bubbling river and passes several broad vistas of farm and forest. The area is popular with local walkers and there are pull-off spots along the roadway if you care to join them.

Upon reaching County Road 8, turn left. You will be suprised to come across one of the Ministry of Natural Resources' secrets, Mono Cliffs Provincial Park. This place is active with Bruce Trail hikers and mountain bikers, and yet, even if the parking lot is full, it's still easy to find a stretch of trail all to yourself. Hike along woodland paths, scramble to the top of the limestone outcrops or enjoy the view over rolling pasture. The wind plays a

beautiful symphony in the pines, a deeply therapeutic respite from city life.

A stone's throw away is Mono Centre, a village that has escaped the worst of the estate development that is rampant in the area. If you need to regain your strength after the park, visit the Mono Cliffs Inn for its famous mussels or the downstairs Peter Cellars for some potent potables and pub food (closed Tuesday and Wednesday). Right next door is a charming building that houses the Cliff Swallow Gallery (local artists), Rural Routes gift shop (dried flowers and fine art) and the Mono Cliffs Trading Company (exotic clothes and gifts).

Head back to Mono Road 3 and drive north. Upon reaching Highway 89, head east to the hamlet of Violet Hill and to Mrs. Mitchell's, a restaurant located in an 1889 schoolhouse. And what a rewarding stop this is, whether for lunch, afternoon tea, dinner or brunch (the latter on weekends only, closed Mondays). The grace of the service is matched by the superb food. Brunch ranges from pecan waffles to crabmeat omelettes, everything served with hot mulled cider and homemade muffins. Dinner includes stuffed pork tenderloin, chicken breast or roast rack of lamb. The decor is country comfortable, with attractive seasonal decorations, stencilled floors and walls, and two fragrant fireplaces. A perfect setting for a country day.

Across the street from Mrs. Mitchell's, in the original Orange Lodge, is Granny Taught Us, with plenty of fabrics, wreaths, Victorian-style nightclothes, rugged sweaters, and the same beautiful wooden floors as the restaurant.

Drive east on Highway 89 to Airport Road and turn south. Ever wonder where Santa and his family spend the summer? It could very well be in the Hockley area, for the fields are full of Christmas trees, from the tiniest sprout to great big granddaddies destined for outdoor displays. If you are

Mrs. Mitchell's

visiting during December (and the Hockley is a fine winter drive), stop to cut your own tree. Hockley Tree Farm and McKenney Trees are only two of the many "you-cut" operations here. Airport Road is also a good drive for skiers, with both downhill and cross-country operations in the vicinity. The downhill runs tend to be short and sweet, but are probably good for keeping you in shape for more adventurous skiing elsewhere.

Continue south on Airport Road. For the last of today's sideroading, take the 5th Sideroad west. This hilly route through scenic farmland eventually joins up with the Hockley Valley Road near Highway 10, right back where you started on this tour of gravel roads and wooden floors.

Mrs. Mitchell's
(519) 925-3627

Mono Cliffs Inn
(519) 941-5109

Mono Cliffs Provincial Park
Daily, year-round

34

ALLISTON
Surprise, Surprise

Just when you thought that you had seen all there was to see in the countryside of central Ontario, here comes a trip that will show you at least one, if not two sites that you have never visited before. Pack a sense of adventure along with your picnic lunch and head into uncharted territory north of Metro Toronto.

Drive north on Highway 400, exit at Highway 89 and go west to Alliston, a quiet farm service community of tree-lined streets and grand red-brick homes. At the west end of town the main street comes to a T junction where you will turn right (north) and follow signs to Canadian Forces Base Borden. Don't be alarmed when approaching the armed guards at the gate, for after a brief sign-in, the base welcomes visitors to the military museum.

At first glance, the Canadian Military Museum is a lot of historic uniforms and aged military paraphernalia in standard glass cases. But look a little closer and you'll find some thought-provoking items among the 10,000 artifacts preserved in several spacious rooms. Especially for those visitors from a generation of Canadians untouched by war, the museum is a reminder of the meaningful role the military has played in shaping Canadian character and identity.

Earl Rowe Provincial Park

Many display pieces bring home the fact that Canadian military involvement (from the Boer War to the present day) has touched the lives of every family. The walls are covered with historic photographs, such as huge classes of graduating university students, all in uniform and ready to leave for Europe. Other photographs are of northern training camps, an expanse of white tents stretching off to the horizon. Base Borden was one of Canada's most important training facilities, and at some point most of the army personnel in WWII spent time here.

The history of several segments of the Canadian military is related in detail: the medical corps, the armoured corps and intelligence and security. Each of these activities are described through equipment, uniforms, and diaries and correspondence. The most gripping exhibits, however, are those which put a human face on military life. For example, the diary of a lonely Canadian soldier stationed in Egypt in 1915. Or the simple survival kit issued to soldiers. This kit contained water-purifying tablets, anti-sleep pills, gum, food, razor blades, and an English-German phrase book. On the whole, it looks frighteningly inadequate for survival in hostile territory.

If you delight in looking at military hardware from past decades, head to the park across the street from the museum to see anti-aircraft guns, tanks, anti-tank guns and armoured personnel carriers. These are mammoth machines—sure to interest children—and they represent countries such as Canada, the United States, Britain, Italy, Germany and Sweden. If you need a Sherman or Centurian tank for your checklist, this is the place for you. In another section of the base is a field of historic aircraft (all post-World War II). Of special interest are the CF-100, Voodoo, Sabre and Tracker aircraft.

And now it's time for something completely different. Head south to Alliston and then west along Highway 89 to Earl Rowe Provincial Park. The park is 317 hectares of rolling fields and woodland, the latter mainly along the Boyne River. There is a 36-hectare lake with fishing and non-motorized boating, a boat rental facility and food concession. The half-hectare swimming pool is a great place to cool off without having to drive far from the city, but be warned that it can get busy on weekends.

Many visitors to Earl Rowe arrive in early spring and late fall to watch trout and salmon battle the current as they migrate upstream. The park has a fish ladder, which is the best spot to watch rainbow trout hurdle up the concrete steps to reach the lake above the dam. Fish biologists are sometimes on duty tagging and measuring the fish as they pass through the ladder. Call the park office to check on the best dates, for the size of the migration varies with weather conditions.

Whatever the season, the footpaths along the Boyne make for easy and pleasant walking or cross-country skiing. Interpretive brochures identify points of interest along the way, such as a hermit's cave. An 1899 schoolhouse stands in the park, a remnant of Meadowbrook, a thriving mill village that stood on what is now park territory.

Ministry of Natural Resources staff work hard to provide recreational facilties for every taste. Baseball, volleyball, soccer and horseshoes equipment and facilities are available for rent. There is a fitness trail with exercise stations in a wooded setting. For the naturalist, there is a full summertime program of guided walks, lectures, films, craft and camping skills workshops, and much more. During the winter (a good time to visit, when the crowds of summer have dispersed), there are ski trails, snowmobiling on roadways, superb tobogganing, and the lake is shovelled for skating.

Next time you're looking for something to do, pack up you troubles in your old kit bag and head for Alliston.

Base Borden Military Museum
Tuesday-Friday 9:00-12:00 and 1:15-3:00
Saturday and Sunday 1:30-4:00
(705) 424-1200

Earl Rowe Provincial Park
park open to public daily,
some facilities operate seasonally
(705) 435-4331

35

BRAMPTON
Peel Back the Decades

An urban ocean of new housing, shopping malls, car manufacturing... That's Brampton, right? Wrong. Downtown Brampton is full of historic homes and public buildings, and it has its own top-notch regional museum. Spend a day discovering the Brampton that the decades have left untouched.

The Peel Heritage Complex, on Wellington Street in the centre of old Brampton, comprises the Peel County Jail and Registry Office. A clever renovation connects the two buildings via a foyer so that the coarse wall of the jail is now actually inside the complex. A narrow concrete cell, lists of typical punishments (lashing, treadmill, incarceration, hard labour), and equipment such as handcuffs and leg shackles are leftovers from when the jail was constructed in 1866. Originally used for criminals, indigents and the ill, the jail of today houses an impressive array of items from Peel's past.

The display begins with the days of the Mississauga Indians and travels through pioneer times to the rapid urbanization of the present century. The most enlightening exhibit presents typical occupations in early Ontario—photographer, cooper, tinsmith, doctor, builder, homemaker—immortalized through implements and products. This museum has one of the better local-history collections in southern Ontario, well worth a visit. The Peel Registry Office is now an art gallery with paintings of the area over many decades, an interesting way to study landscape changes. The Heritage Complex gift shop sells quality books, jewellery and craft items.

History is not confined to the Heritage Complex, for it is laid in brick and mortar throughout downtown Brampton. It is not difficult to imagine away the decades while walking along quiet, shady streets lined with elegant homes. Ask at the Complex for a walking-tour brochure. Head out the front door of the Heritage Complex and left around the corner for a good look at the County Courthouse.

This stately yellow-brick building with its unusual domed tower is so perfectly romantic that it has appeared in several films. Like the jail, the courthouse dates to 1866 and was designed by William Kaufman.

Walk east on Wellington and turn left onto Chapel Street. Notice the decorated bargeboards on many of the homes. The original fire hall is on Chapel near Queen. Like most fire halls of the mid-1800s, it has a tower which was used for drying hoses. The Board of Trade is housed in the Carnegie Library (1907) and presents a charming face to the street.

Cross Queen Street and head to the mill at the corner of Queen and Union streets. A century-old planing mill turned knitting mill has again changed forms: it is now offices, a restaurant and brew pub. Houston's serves steak and seafood as well as a hearty Sunday brunch in an old-time setting. Tracks brews its own "Old Mill" ale and lager according to old German methods and offers a good selection of pub grub, from ploughman's lunch to Cajun wings.

Head west along Queen to another popular eatery, O'Malley's, located in the original post office of 1889. This impressive building is faced with Credit Valley stone (you may recognize it as the same stone used in the Ontario Legislature and Toronto's Old City Hall) and was designed by Thomas Fuller, who was also responsible for the first Parliament Buildings in Ottawa. O'Malley's serves burgers, pasta and sandwiches in a setting of polished brass and wrought iron.

Walk or drive north on Main Street for a glimpse at what were Brampton's most impressive homes at the time the post office and courthouse were built. Take a detour east on Church, north on Union, and return to Main along Alexander. Victorian homes like to wear their decoration on the outside, so check out the exceptional workmanship on the eaves and the door and window surrounds.

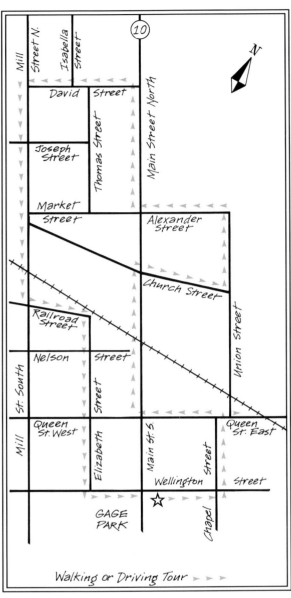

Brampton

This area looks much as it did at the turn of the century.

Continue north on Main Street. Take note of numbers 173, 198 and 204, which are good examples of Brampton's well-kept historic homes. Turn left onto David Street. Don't miss the house on the corner, the most unusual house in the area, with not a 90-degree angle in it. The charm of David Street is well preserved and includes a few small "Ontario cottages" popular in the mid-1800s. These single-storey homes with steep central gables are one of Ontario's contributions to the world of architecture.

Travel south on Mill Street. This neighbourhood built up around the rail station is typical of working-class neighbourhoods at the turn of the century. Conclude the tour of yesteryear by enjoying Gage Park at the corner of Main and Wellington. It has long been prominent in the public life of Brampton, with concerts and special events during the summer. The park is watched over by a mansion called Haggertlea (1870), which was the hub of Brampton social life, just as the Haggert foundry was the hub of Brampton business life.

A visit to one of Ontario's fastest-growing communities is an opportunity to enjoy a meal in historic surroundings, appreciate Victorian street scenes, and visit a top-notch museum. Peel back the decades in Brampton.

Peel Heritage Complex
Tuesday-Sunday 12:00-4:30
Thursday 12:00-4:30 and 6:00-9:00
(416) 451-9051

36

KLEINBURG
The Conserver Society

The conserver society, a commonly heard term during the last decade, describes the kind of changes needed in ethics and lifestyles in order to avoid "ecotastrophe". On the outskirts of sprawling, smoggy Toronto lies Kleinburg, a village that's home to three diverse approaches to conservation.

The Kortright Centre for Conservation is a 400-hectare natural area with an imaginative staff who are devoted to spreading the word about energy efficiency and nature conservation. The nature centre is a lively place with interesting hands-on activities related to the themes of water, energy and wildlife. The programs vary with the season: owl prowls, a kite festival and a water magician in March; bird-feeder building, battery-free toys and snow ecology around Christmastime. The exhibit area of the nature centre offers practical ideas for conservation in the home and cottage, such as water-saving devices and window warmers. There's also a movie theatre, café (complete with a pileated woodpecker at the window), picnic area and a shop with gifts for that "green" person on your list. Activities, exhibits and movies are geared towards kids, making Kortright one of the best family outings around Toronto. The centre and some of the trails are wheelchair accessible.

Outdoors the Kortright Centre has 12 kilometres of hiking and cross-country skiing trails in rugged valley land with boardwalks and lookouts. The forest is magnificent, with huge trees of 34 species, scores of birds and even deer. The Power Trip trail has exhibits on solar energy and wind power, and a poplar plantation for biomass production. (Kortright supplies wind-generated electricity to the Ontario Hydro grid.) There are trails with wildlife shrubs and an apiary (two million buzzers generate Kortright's own honey, available for sale).

To reach the Kortright Centre from Metro Toronto, take Highway 400 north to Major Mackenzie Drive, head west to Pine Valley Drive, and drive south about 1 kilometre. The route is signposted. After picking up a few pointers on making your home environment-friendly, drive into the town of Kleinburg by heading west along Major Mackenzie and then north at Islington Avenue.

At the south end of town is the renowned McMichael Canadian Art Collection, where the great wilderness is preserved for all time on canvas. McMichael is home to a huge collection by the Group of Seven and their contemporaries—over 2,000 works in all. The collection also features paintings and sculpture by Native artists from across the nation. A good selection of work is available in the gift shop.

The McMichael Collection is housed in a remarkable building, a striking construction of fieldstone and rough-hewn log that is grand and rustic at the same time. The galleries have huge expanses of glass so that the visitor can turn from wilderness on canvas to a view overlooking steep valley lands (all the more beautiful during autumn). Visitors are invited to hike, ski or picnic on the grounds. There's also a restaurant and summertime dining patio.

Kortright taught us about the three R's—reduce, reuse and recycle. Drive into Kleinburg for a pleasant dose of recycling, consumer-style. Pretty well everything that's part of Ontario's cultural heritage is for sale in town, from dolls to furniture to currant buns. Kleinburg's shops and eateries are housed in well-preserved historic buildings, making it a good town for those interested in architectural conservation.

Antique-hunting is good at the Martin Gordon Gallery, Lilac Bush Antiques and Kaiser House Antiques. Fine reproductions of old Ontario furniture in oak and pine are found at Whispering Pines. Everything you need to complete a country interior can be found at the Side Door, from collector birdseed containers to cotton rugs. Head for the Jeremy workshop in the restored general store and post office,

McMichael Gallery

where jewellers Watson and Aspinall design pieces of unusual beauty (closed Mondays).

Kleinburg has a good variety of eating places geared to every budget. At one end of the spectrum is the Doctor's House and Livery, which indeed sits on the same spot as the original town doctor's stable. The Doctor's House and Livery is well known for early Ontario foods such as pheasant and duckling, as well as a popular Sunday brunch (reservations advisable). At the casual and inexpensive end of the spectrum are two tea shops, Mr. McGregor's House and the Kleinburg Mews Tea Room. Both serve light meals and have wonderful sweet tables. Flowers for My Daughters has a reputation for fresh foods inventively prepared. The menu is a lively combination of tastes (reviewers label it Thai-Caribbean-Mediterranean) and may include pumpkin-ginger soup, pasta with prawns, and chicken jerk. The prices are as inviting as the friendly ambience.

A daytrip to Kleinburg goes a long way to moving us towards a society that cares for our natural environment and cultural heritage—a conserver society.

Kortright Centre
Daily 10:00-4:00
(416) 832-2289

McMichael Canadian Art Collection
April-October:
Daily 10:00-5:00
November-March:
Tuesday-Sunday 11:00-4:30
(416) 893-1121

37

MISSISSAUGA
Life in the Slow Lane

The next time you're zooming along the Queen Elizabeth Way through vast modern Mississauga, take a break from the hectic pace and visit several places custom-made for slowing down and relishing life. Hike along a river valley, dine at a stone inn and visit a pioneer homestead. All this and more awaits the traveller willing to leave the highway.

Adopt a more human pace of life by visiting nineteenth-century Ontario at the Bradley House Museum. Exit the QEW at Southdown Road south. Drive east along Lakeshore Road and south along Meadow Wood Road (in the town of Clarkson). The museum is at the intersection of Meadow Wood and Orr Road. The Bradley House Museum comprises two 1830s homes and outbuildings, and welcomes you with demonstrations, tours and workshops.

Begin in the simple frame cabin, once home to the Lewis Turner Bradley family and still furnished in the 1830 to 1850 period. Visitors listen with interest as guides describe home life in the days before video, electric lights and telephones, a world of whale-oil lamps, corn-husk dolls, and visits from the Methodist circuit rider. Economy was the order of the day. For example, the kitchen hearth fire was not allowed to die out for ten years because the matches needed for relighting were too expensive. Young visitors ooh with delight when they find out that the Bradley children bathed only five times a year and washed their hair much less often then that—not surprising when you learn that for most of the year the room used for bathing was only five degrees warmer than the outside air.

The Anchorage, an attractive Regency cottage, is under renovation and when complete will provide space for displays on local history, a gift shop and tearoom. The Bradley House currently sells an interesting collection of books and inexpensive kids toys made from pioneer designs.

Drive to Lakeshore Boulevard and head east through Port Credit. Turn north on Mississauga Road. It's time to slow down and do a home and garden tour, since Mississauga Road is a display of the best and biggest in suburban housing. From modest post-war retreats to palatial designer homes in a multitude of styles, Mississauga Road displays them all on well-groomed treed lots.

Continue northbound until Collegeway, then turn west. Just around the bend in the road lies striking Glenerin, a stone-and-cedar mansion overlooking the steep valley of Sawmill Creek. The Glenerin provides accommodation and conference facilities, and more importantly for the daytripper, the inn's Thatcher's Restaurant is a good spot for lunch before hitting the trails. Light lunches are available on Saturdays, and on Sundays there is a buffet brunch. During good weather, the patio offers dining with a valley view. The Glenerin has an unusual history. Built in the 1920s as a country retreat, this handsome building has also been used as a dormitory for English schoolgirls, a convalescent home for executives, and a training school for priests.

After lunch, follow the footpaths near the roadway down into the river valley. (If you are not visiting the Glenerin, parking is limited in the area. Try either Erindale College or the sidestreets along Collegeway.) The forest contains stately examples of trees uncommon in cities, such as shagbark hickory, black walnut, red oak, white pine and butternut. The rushing stream, abundant wildflowers and ferns, vivid fall colour and limestone outcrops provide ample photo opportunities.

Drive south on Mississauga Road, returning to Port Credit (head east along Lakeshore Road). The Port's harbour area is very busy these days, thanks to a revival of Lake Ontario sport-fishing. Coho and chinook salmon, and lake and rainbow trout support a $50-million-a-year industry. Charter fishing operators are available at Port Credit harbour, each offering an invigorating day of fishing, complete with bait and loads of high-tech gear,

Glenerin Inn

for about $60 a person. But it's not necessary to charter a boat and skipper to catch fish in Port Credit. The rod-and-reel gang head for various spots along the lower Credit, including Memorial Park in downtown Port Credit (access from Lakeshore Road). The Credit River downstream of the QEW and Lake Ontario are open to trout and salmon fishing all year; fish sanctuary areas on more northerly parts of the river are closed to fall and winter fishing. Even if fishing is not your bag, Memorial Park is a good place to put up your feet and relax in the fresh breezes off the lake.

If you have left lunching until now, wander in Port Credit for a restaurant that suits. One of the most interesting menus is that of the Dutch Kitchen, housed in an 1850s building topped with, appropriately, a Dutch roof. Traditional favourites such as Indonesian *nasi goreng* combine with European-style desserts

featuring apples and almonds. The service is in the friendly style typical of Port Credit, which has retained its small-town atmosphere despite the encroaching city.

When you have finished touring Port Credit, you can return to the QEW and head for home, certainly more refreshed and peaceful.

Bradley House Museum
April to mid-December:
Tuesday to Friday 10:00-4:00
Saturday and Sunday 1:00-5:00
hours will change beginning
in spring 1992
(416) 822-4884

Glenerin Inn (restaurant)
(416) 828-7449

38

KING CITY
Jewel in the Crown

Of all the rural townships surrounding Metro Toronto, King Township to the northwest stands alone as the most beautiful. It has more grand historic homes and wide vistas of countryside than any other township. But the jewel in this crown is the Lady Eaton estate, custom-made for a day of outdoor exploring and fine dining.

The Lady Eaton estate, now part of Seneca College, is located on the west side of Dufferin Street north of King Road (an exit off Highway 400). Three hundred hectares of rolling farmland and forest were purchased by department-store magnate Sir John Eaton in 1920 and used as a summertime retreat. The estate was also used to grow all the fresh flowers sold in Eaton's stores. Palatial Eaton Hall was constructed during the 1930s and used by Lady Eaton until 1971; after her death, the property was purchased by the college.

The Lady Eaton estate is perhaps best known as a great place to cross-country ski. Seneca College offers midweek and weekend lessons (sign up by calling the continuing education office) and ski rentals for those attending courses. Twenty kilometres of groomed trails are open to the public when not in use for instruction. Call the college for times or listen to the radio ski reports. Even if you are not a skier, the wintertime walking is wonderful on forest paths or the college roadways.

Don't assume that the Lady Eaton Estate is only active during the winter, for the college offers courses in sailing and canoeing during the summer. Summer hiking on the campus is rewarding because the area is remarkably quiet, leaving the visitor to appreciate the waters of Marie Lake twinkling through the trees and the masses of spring and summer wildflowers. The campus is a good place to find birds, deer and other wildlife.

On to Eaton Hall. This 72-room stone chateau stands at the north end of the lake amid a large coniferous forest. Sir Henry Pellatt of

Casa Loma fame helped in the design of Eaton Hall, and it shows: plenty of turrets, a massive stone fireplace, a panelled library and a fountain. Eaton Hall is open for lunch and dinner (reservations essential, check ahead for schedule). Lunch may be from the menu or buffet, depending on how many guests are being served. And what a buffet it is—dozens of salads, very appealing hot dishes and an incredible choice of sweets are spread on tables filling the entire great hall. Quality and quantity to please everyone. Dinner is always table-service, with entrees such as Cornish hen, prime rib or veal cordon bleu. Diners have terrific views of the gardens and lake from the large dining room, the bar-lounge or the round zodiac room with its gilded ceiling murals of the astrological signs. Christmastime is very special, with much effort put into decking the halls with boughs of spruce and metres of red ribbon (and of course dinners with plum pudding for dessert).

Eaton Hall is home to Seneca's training centre for business managers, providing accommodation, meals and recreational facilities for conferences. The hall is also part of the college program, providing a place for students in hospitality and tourism courses to gain practical experience. What a place to go to school!

Although at some point we must say goodbye to Lady Eaton's summer hunting grounds, we can be grateful that this spot is not all that is delightful in King Township. Spend some time in King City, located at the junction of King Road and Keele Street. (Drive south from the Lady Eaton estate and go west on King Road.)

Crawford Wells General Store was constructed in 1863, and it has changed so little since then that it has been used as a movie set. Piety Ridge Primitives and Sheena's Kitchen share space here now, and it's worth a visit just to appreciate the old-time cash register and display cases. The wares sold in a country store haven't changed much in almost a

Eaton Hall

century and a half: an eclectic assortment of nightshirts, dolls, dried flowers, craft supplies, crockery, furniture and gourmet foods. This country atmosphere extends to the restaurant area, which serves homemade goodies such as pecan tarts and chocolate-chip cookies.

King City has another eatery of renown, charming red-brick Hogan's Inn. The food in the formal dining room and the warm atmosphere of the country pub garner high praise from reviewers (reservations suggested). This small village has two outstanding art galleries. The Whitten Gallery beside the general store sells original art, often bright and light-hearted in theme, from a variety of painters and sculptors. The Tomas Gallery on King Road just east of Keele has an impressive collection of prints from Bateman, Romance and Doolittle, to name but a few.

First-rate hiking, fine dining in a picturesque mansion, a real country store, fine art, and the magnificent Lady Eaton estate await the traveller in King Township.

Eaton Hall
(416) 833-4500

Seneca College
(416) 833-3333

Hogan's Inn
(416) 833-5311

39

BRADFORD
Marsh March

One of Ontario's most familiar landmarks is also one of its most unusual landscapes. The Holland Marsh is familiar to Torontonians as the flat expanse which reveals itself just north of the Highway 9 exit on Highway 400. This jet-black and lively green carpet nestled in the hills surrounding Bradford is a welcome sign that the city is indeed well behind and cottage life lies just ahead. But few travellers take the time to investigate the Holland Marsh more closely and thus fail to appreciate its blend of native marsh and human settlement.

The Holland Marsh is a long ellipse centred on the Holland River, extending from near Schomberg in the southwest to Cook's Bay (on Lake Simcoe) in the northeast. Begin the day by travelling west from Highway 400 about 2 kilometres on Highway 9. The first stops are Highway 9 Market and Don's Fruit and Vegetables. Plan a visit for when the

Holland Marsh   —photo by Donna Carpenter

produce is freshest, from June to October. The Holland Marsh has made Ontario famous as a producer of carrots and onions, and both these crops are available in many varieties. Tomatoes, potatoes and lettuce are also grown in abundance, and local markets offer these in addition to imported crops.

Continue westerly 1/2 kilometre and turn right onto West Canal Road. Secluded West Canal Road, brushed by overhanging willows, provides the most scenic tour of the marsh. On the one side there is the languid green canal, the surface broken only by the plunge of a kingfisher. On the other side there are undeviating rows of vegetables reaching from the very edge of the asphalt to the hills in the distance. The fields are dotted with the hunched forms of planters or pickers, each wearing an Oriental straw hat as protection from the merciless Ontario sun. Occasionally a truck heavily laden with lettuce, crawls towards you, tilting under its green tresses.

The fields are so productive that it comes as a surprise that the Holland Marsh was completely undeveloped until very recently. The first Dutch settlers, about 15 families, arrived here between 1925 and 1930. By applying drainage and gardening skills evolved in Europe, as well as co-operative management schemes, they became the first settlers to successfully farm the marsh. About 2,800 hectares of marsh are now under cultivation, a very small area to be feeding Toronto.

Follow West Canal Road under the 400 all the way to Highway 11 and Bradford. Where the Holland River meets Highway 11 is a favourite locale with fishermen. Bring a rod and reel and join your buddies along the canal. Local fishing legends describe gargantuan pike of the Holland Marsh area. At the south end of town on Highway 11 are two large vegetable markets. From glossy watermelons to sweet cider, Oak Ridges and Bak's sell it all. If you are picnicking, load up here and at one of Bradford's delis on Highway 11. If you want a longer stop in town, across from the markets is the Bullfrog Restaurant. Fresh local produce is the attraction here, with rhubarb and raspberries making it from garden to dessert in a matter of hours (open daily).

Continue north through Bradford along Highway 11. Turn right at the 9th Line to reach the Scanlon Creek Conservation Area. This 283-hectare day-use park is a good place for a picnic, with nature trails, a small beach and fishing.

Retrace your path to Highway 11 and head north again. Turn east along the 12th Line in order to have a close-up look at what the entire Holland Marsh region might have looked like before drainage and market gardening. Ducks Unlimited, the Ministry of Natural Resources and the South Lake Simcoe Conservation Authority jointly manage 578 hectares of marsh known as the Holland Marsh Provincial Wildlife Area. This area is especially precious, since it is one of southern Ontario's largest remaining wetlands and one of our marshes least degraded by human activity.

The 12th Line ends at a parking lot with a trail to a boardwalk that leads right through the bulrushes and cat-tails to a viewing tower. The view over the marsh allows a study of several popular techniques of managing wetlands for wildlife, such as open areas of water (potholes), artificial islands for nesting waterfowl, and dikes for controlling water levels. There are also trails and viewing areas along the 11th Line, which is a good spot to launch a canoe for a really intimate look at the marsh. Even from the shoreline, there are terrific opportunities to spot heron, coot, teal, marsh wrens or some lesser-known residents such as Caspian and least terns, leopard frogs and a variety of butterflies.

Spend a day exploring the split personality of the Holland Marsh, simultaneously a wildlife refuge and a market garden.

40

NEWMARKET
A Temple That Lieth Foursquare

North of Newmarket, just off the beaten track, stands the Sharon Temple. Not only is the temple a remarkable building, but it is at the centre of a fascinating story of individual achievement. Architecture, history and a powerful sense of place combine to make Sharon a rewarding day adventure. The Sharon Temple is on Leslie Street a few kilometres north of Newmarket.

Our story begins when David Willson emigrated from New York State to the Newmarket area in the early 1800s. A Presbyterian turned Quaker, charismatic and visionary Willson parted from the Quakers and founded the Children of Peace in 1812. The Children of Peace grew from five families to a congregation of over 200 within a generation. The Children of Peace combined Judaic and Christian elements with a large dose of Eastern mysticism in their religious beliefs. Their daily life included formal and vocational training for both men and women, a music school, a meeting house and the temple.

A guided tour of the temple and grounds is a must, for the guides are not only well versed in their topic, but overflow with enthusiasm for this unique building and its history. July is a very special time to visit the temple, as the annual Music at Sharon brings a quality program of vocal and instrumental performances. The first Friday of September recreates the Children's annual evening ceremony, in which all 2,592 windows of the temple are illuminated by candles. Advance reservations are required for Music at Sharon and the Illuminations.

The guided tours begin with the temple, which resembles a three-storey wedding cake with dark-green trim. But this is not a flight of fancy, it is the expression in wood of religious principles. The three storeys represent the Trinity; the square floor plan, the desire to deal squarely with all men; each of the four doors represents a point of the compass, indicating that all people enter as equals; and 12 columns represent the Apostles. Music

was a key element in Willson's theology, and inside is the first Canadian-made organ. The temple was used only 15 times a year, when members would march to the temple for alms-giving, with band, choir and banners.

The method of construction was also unusual. The temple was built in pieces off-site (in seven years, like Solomon's temple) and assembled at Sharon so that the site would not be disturbed. The Children of Peace put a premium on excellence of craftsmanship, and this is evident in the temple, which is built without caulking. Imagine how miraculous the temple must have seemed, built in the backwoods at a time when roads were mere trails and wolves howled at night.

There are several other buildings on the premises. The 1819 home of Ebenezer Doan is a charming Georgian frame house replete with picket fence. That it is a model of fine workmanship is entirely appropriate, since Doan was the master builder of the temple. Every convenience of the period is built in, such as walk-in closets and pantry, and an ornate fire box and humidifier. The kitchen area includes clever time-savers of yesteryear, such as sausage stuffers and steam irons. An authentic period herb garden is included in the yard.

The drive shed houses displays on the history of the temple. Most intriguing is a modern-day miracle, the discovery of papers hidden for 158 years within the Ark in the Temple. On May 1, 1990, during restoration of the Ark, a secret compartment was discovered; the compartment contained 11 books of manuscript from David Willson himself, hundreds of pages, including his most private thoughts on leaving the Quakers. The entire process of discovery and results are on display.

The Sharon Temple grounds also include a log cabin which illustrates the typical "first home" used by York County pioneers. It contains a large collection of wool winders,

Interior, Sharon Temple

looms and spinning wheels. Volunteers use the cabin for demonstrations of cooking, spinning, caning and weaving. The delightful little building to the front of the temple was a study given to David Willson by his followers, a replica of their meeting house.

If the peace of the temple has you wishing for some solitude in the countryside, take heart, for there is a quiet picnic site nearby. Drive south from the temple. En route note Maplebyrn, a dark board-and-batten house built in 1852; it features an interesting panelled doorway. Walnut Farm, which dates to 1857, is just south of Maplebyrn. Many of the Children of Peace, including David Willson, were interred in the Sharon Burying Ground on Leslie Street.

Turn right (west) at Green Lane (about 2 kilometres south of the temple). Continue west for almost 3 kilometres until you reach tiny and quiet Rogers Reservoir Conservation Area. For the naturalist, there are nature trails through marsh and field. The park also includes sections of the Newmarket Canal which was built during the early years of this century to carry boats from Lake Simcoe to Newmarket. Although built, the canal was never used.

A daytrip to the Sharon Temple acts an as antidote to modern life in two ways. Our faith in the power of the individual to make a difference is restored, and we enjoy a short rest from the hectic pace of the city. Long live the Sharon Temple.

Sharon Temple
May-October:
Daily 10:00-5:00
(416) 478-2389

41

AURORA
Spring Fling

Ontarians wait patiently through a long winter of sleet, slush and sombre skies. Fortunately, the wait is rewarded with the natural celebration that is Ontario springtime—the rich sweetness of maple syrup, a flash of colour as a trout moves upstream, the rhythm of a robin's song. When spring madness hits your household and itchy feet long for an outing, fill a day with pancake breakfasts, spring fishing and plans for the home garden.

The first harbinger of spring in Ontario is a longer day, so start a spring fling early, having breakfast at Bruce's Mill Conservation Area. Drive north on Highway 404 and then east on the Stouffville Road about 3 kilometres to Bruce's Mill. From mid-March to mid-April Bruce's Mill is the site of maple syrup demonstrations, the maple trees being tapped and sap boiled according to three methods:

Indian style, pioneer style, and modern sap line and evaporator. The concession serves pancake, sausage and maple syrup breakfasts. Sitting outside savouring pancakes and the scent of wood fires, face cooled by March air yet warmed by the sun, is a distinctive pleasure of Ontario spring. There are plenty of nature trails if you need to walk off some of the pancakes. If the snow cover permits, Bruce's Mill has 17 kilometres of groomed cross-country ski trails (with rentals and instruction). The millpond is cleared for winter skating, although by March the season may be over. The century-and-a-half-old mill is open for tours in spring and summer, and the trillium display in the woods is ready for inspection in late spring.

Continue east on Stouffville Road to Highway 48. It is a short drive north to Burd's Trout

Sheppard's Bush Conservation Area

Fishing. No fishin' hole ever guaranteed the action you'll find at Burd's stocked fish ponds, open daily from mid-March through to freeze up in late fall. There's a modest admission fee, and the fish (rainbow trout and salmon) are priced per ounce. The limit is five fish per rod, and it's not hard to meet your limit. There's a concession stand that also offers rod rentals (bait included); all you need to bring is good luck. This is a very popular spot for family and company picnics. Be the first one on your block to bring home a spring trout. (For a real fishy story, visit the Ringwood Fish Culture Station just north of Burd's on Highway 48. Displays explain the business of raising salmon and trout and releasing them to repopulate Ontario's streams.)

Drive north on Highway 48 to the Aurora Road (Wellington Street) and head west. If you slept in and missed breakfast at Bruce's Mill, then you can recoup your pride by enjoying the weekend pancake lunches put on by the Aurora Lions club at Sheppard's Bush Conservation Area. Just west of Bayview Avenue, drive south on Industry Street to the park. As with Bruce's Mill, there are displays of old-style and modern methods of syrup production. If you've been in hibernation and missed maple syrup season altogether, the spring flowers make Sheppard's Bush worth a May visit.

Springtime is also garden time and the Aurora area has two shops that will give you a garden like no other. Continue west on Wellington, past downtown to Temperance Street. Turn south to Aimer's Wildflower Seeds. Aimer's have built a wide reputation on wildflower seeds and bulbs, selling packaged seed according to species and collections of seed designed to meet special needs. The latter are sold in attractive cans or bags, categorized according to colour, scent, environment (sun or shade), or use (gardens for hummingbirds, butterflies, children or even edible flowers). One inexpensive can may produce 30,000 blooms from spring to fall. The shop includes books, plant food, terracotta pots, dried flowers, and calendars. There's expert advice on starting a wildflower garden, a great way to green-up your household, get your yard off drugs, and save time and money.

But a garden is not all flowers and ground cover. Orchestrate the home landscape for sound and movement by providing some wildlife habitat. To find out how, make tracks for Birdlife Services in Thornhill. Drive south along Yonge Street, turn right on Centre Street, immediately right onto Old Yonge Street, and continue until you reach Birdlife Services. What a find for nature lovers, veteran and novice alike. Start with the bird houses, picking the one designed for the bird you want in your yard: a kestrel box perhaps, a bluebird or chickadee box, or how about a robin nesting platform? Don't miss the great selection of bird feed in economical mixes or in specialty bags for the feathered connoisseur who will only touch a particular variety of sunflower seed or peanut. Feeders are available in dozens of models, including hummingbird and oriole feeders complete with syrup mixes. There are also lots of equipment for deterring squirrels, and you'll find a good collection of bird-feeding books and guides, recordings, prints, photographs, clothing and other paraphernalia for the bird brain in your family.

Mother Nature makes an Ontario spring like no other. Where else could you have newly boiled syrup for breakfast, freshly caught trout for lunch, and be home in time to erect a purple martin house in the backyard? Ontario spring: definitely worth the wait.

Bruce's Mill Conservation Area
Hours vary seasonally, generally
Daily to dusk
(416) 661-6600 (administration)
(416) 887-5531 (site)

Burd's Trout Fishing
Mid-March to fall freeze-up
Daily 8:00-dusk
(416) 640-2928

Sheppard's Bush Conservation Area
Daily to dusk
(416) 895-1281

Birdlife Services
Monday-Friday 9:00-5:30
Saturday 9:00-5:00
Closed Mondays June-September
(416) 221-2473

Aimer's Seeds
Monday-Saturday 9:00-5:00
(416) 833-5282

42

UNIONVILLE
Miracle on Main Street

Aah, for the perfect daytrip destination, that harmonious blend of shopping, dining and community events. Unionville, just northeast of Toronto at Highway 7 and Kennedy Road, is one town that has achieved such a model combination of attractions and is reaping the reward of a thriving tourist industry.

Although Unionville is beset by country clubs and subdivisions, it has a distinctly charming atmosphere because its nineteenth-century buildings have been lovingly restored and provided with a frame of lush curbside plantings. The history buff has a great opportunity to study the street scene typically found in Ontario villages of 100 years ago. The board-and-batten post office and general store (1849) is now Muriel's Flowers. The Queens Hotel was the centre of village life during the mid-1800s, serving as inn, dance hall and council chambers. Religious life centred on the Congregational Church (1879), First Presbyterian (near the corner of Carlton Road and Main Street, 1862) and a Congregational meeting house (1847) that now houses the

Stonemill Bakehouse. And there are many examples of buildings in the Romantic style, decorated with shutters and gingerbreading. The oldest house in town? Well, that's the Stiver House, built of adobe in 1829.

Unionville has shops galore, and each one is committed to the top end of the market in merchandise and price. For antique buffs, the Jug & Basin specializes in silver, glassware and china (Limoges a house specialty). Looking for the unusual? Try the Stiver House for terra-cotta bird bottles that are replicas of those used in early Williamsburg, as well as an excellent selection of early Canadian harvest tables and hutches. That special lace, rag rug or fabric needed to complete an early Ontario decor may be found at the Queen's Pantry.

One of the most striking buildings on Main Street is the original fire hall, constructed in 1933. It currently houses Old Firehall Sports, selling sports equipment and clothes. Also for the outdoorsy is Hiker's Haven, with the best

Unionville

Unionville Planing Mill

in adventure equipment, from canoes to sleeping bags (now called sleeping systems) to biodegradable soap and dried foods.

Unionville is the perfect place to do your holiday shopping all year round. Two Pine Doors offers country-style gift items such as a wide selection of Anne of Green Gables toiletries for fans of Avonlea. Head for Diana's Miniatures and Craft Boutique for dolls, doll houses and accessories. From fine china to reproduction wallpaper, these dolls live better than most shoppers. And last, but not least, are the clothiers, ranging from quality casual gear to Mariani's custom-made and European apparel.

There are several gift shops and art galleries located in the Planing Mill. This was the site of White's Mill (1873), and although the original building was destroyed by fire in 1983, this reproduction is a good complement to old Main Street. White's Mill Trading Company has a wide range of gifts, from specialty books to crafts, as does the Victorian Parlour. The Elizabeth Gallery sells paintings and prints ranging from Romance and Bateman to an interesting collection of street scenes from old Ontario.

Even the most ardent shopper will have had their fill of Unionville's commercial treasures at some point, and that is the time to enjoy a good meal. Two restaurants that have wide

followings are the Unionville House and the Old Country Inn. The Unionville House, in a charming 130-year- old residence with a pretty country garden out front, serves well-prepared French cooking. The Old Country Inn provides ample portions of goulash and schnitzel. Save room for dessert, for there are lots of mouth-watering sweets at the Dessert Peddler, Livingwater Restaurant & Cafe Gallery (in the Planing Mill) and the Stonemill Bakehouse.

Unionville has a score of weekend events. Most noteworthy is the Village Festival in early June, two days of parades, contests, bake and craft sales, music and a petting zoo. Unionville's Old Tyme Christmas will melt even the Scroogiest among us. With stores open extra late, you can enjoy gift buying amid sparkling decorations and carollers, and have free cider and popcorn.

If you need a break from creature comforts, head for the parkland along the river. In summer there's sailboarding on Toogood Pond, and in winter there are cross-country ski rentals from Old Firehall Sports.

Whether you're a born-again shopper or simply enjoy strolling through a well-preserved town from the last century, a day in Unionville can be as busy or as relaxed as you choose.

43

MARKHAM
Country Style

If you haven't noticed, country is "in." From home decorating to clothing to cooking, everyone is striving for an authentic rural Ontario look. How ironic that one of the best places to achieve that look is in a wealthy and fast-growing bedroom community—Markham.

Start an old Ontario day by experiencing the real thing at the Markham District Historical Museum located on Main Street (Highway 48) about 2 1/2 kilometres north of Highway 7. This is a large museum, with about two dozen buildings on 10 hectares. From mid-June to mid-September there are guided tours of the buildings; the rest of the year you can wander the grounds and take self-guided tours through selected buildings. The museum really hums with activity on the special-event days in June, September and October (call museum staff for details).

The Markham Museum staff are justifiably proud of the recently completed land transportation exhibit ("The Road Taken, 1794-1900"), housed in a spacious building (open all year). Historic documents, photographs, colourful dioramas, and a host of artifacts are expertly co-ordinated to explain the critical role roadways played in the social and economic development of Ontario. Learn about the heated political debate over plank versus macadam roads; find out why the settlers' social life flourished during the winter, and how a system of secondary rural roads developed as a means of avoiding toll gates; explore the golden age of the carriage in Markham and learn how carriage-makers adapted to cope with the disastrous impact of railways and automobiles on their business and community.

A wander around the museum grounds is very pleasant, whether the buildings are open for tours or not. Most buildings date to the mid- nineteenth century. There is a small red-brick Baptist Church (available for weddings) and a railway station complete with train (a hit with kids). There is a large number of homes in the museum, and it is interesting to note the changes in size and construction over the decades as families increased their wealth. There is a log cabin, a board-and-batten Mennonite house and a Loyalist plank house. Typical pioneer economic activities are represented by a cider mill, harness shop, butcher shop, sawmill and general store.

If you are visiting Markham during the winter, take the opportunity to visit one of southern Ontario's hidden delights: Cedarena. If you have a Canadian soul that thrills to the rasp of blade on ice and longs to skate al fresco, then look no further. Skate in the centre of an aromatic cedar woods and warm up at the hot chocolate concession—a winter tradition linking families over the centuries. Cedarena is located southeast of the Markham Historical Museum; drive east on Highway 7 and south on the 10th Concession. Cedarena is on the 10th Concession between 14th Avenue and Steeles Avenue. (Keep you eyes peeled for the small sign.)

If you are eager to bring the country village atmosphere of the Markham Museum into your home, then head for Cullen Country Barns. The Barns are located at Steeles Avenue and Kennedy Road (drive south to Steeles and head west).

The Cullen Country Barns are a country shopping experience. The gigantic structure is three floors of natural woodwork gleaned from a dozen barns found on the Pickering airport site. The Barns are filled to the rustic rafters with gifts, clothing for the entire family, stationery and party goods, books, antiques, fabrics and craft supplies—all with a country theme. The merchandise is of the highest quality and the service is friendly and personal. The only problem with the Cullen Country Barns is knowing where to begin. Don't worry, management has come to your aid with maps and guides.

But the Barns are not just shopping. The main-floor Weall & Cullen Garden Centre

Markham Museum

sells plants, fresh flowers, garden tools, and gifts for the green-thumb. The Markham Room provides country-style foods (pot pie, ribs and fruit crumble); the Milliken Room serves buffet breakfast and lunch. Len's General Store has a Fortnum & Mason corner if you fancy Dograpper English mustard or McNeill's apricot preserves. The coffee bar has a good selection of baked goods and candies.

The list of special events and courses offered at the Cullen Country Barns makes it a shopping experience with a difference. A small sample includes stained-glass and quilting workshops, children's magic shows, and lectures on travel, architecture and antiques. The Barns gear up for Christmas in mid-November, with gigantic trimmed trees, a zillion lights and breakfast with Santa—even the most blasé kid will be awed. Last but not least, the Barns have an active lunch and dinner-theatre program. And if all that is not enough, the Barns are surrounded by a shopping mall with even more offerings—but that's another story.

Whether it's a museum glass collection, a country skating rink or a quilting bee, Markham lays it on for us, country style.

Markham District Historical Museum
Mid-June to mid-September:
Tuesday-Saturday 10:00-5:00
Sunday 1:00-5:00
(all buildings)
Mid-September to mid-June:
Tuesday-Sunday 1:00-5:00
(selected buildings only)
(416) 294-4576

Cedarena
December to March, weather permitting
Tuesday (adults only), Thursday
and Saturday 7:30-10:00
Sunday 2:00-4:00
(416) 294-0038

Cullen Country Barns
Stores and Markham Room open daily
(416) 477-4475 (stores and dinner theatre)
(416) 477-1106 (restaurants)

44

STOUFFVILLE
Shop Till You Drop

Do you look upon shopping as a necessary chore or a dreadful bore? Do you avoid spending money (deep pockets and short arms) or refrain from banal browsing? Maybe it's time to change your habits and try a trip to Stouffville's Sales Barn, the shopping experience of a lifetime. To find the Sales Barn, take Highway 48 north from Highway 401 and then head east along Highway 47. Continue through the town of Stouffville and follow Highway 47 when it turns north. You can't miss the huge silver barn, the site of a combination flea, antique and farmers' market that has made Stouffville a regular habit for thousands of shoppers.

The huge central barn is encompassed by hectare upon hectare of tarmac. And that tarmac is covered, as far as the eye can see, by row upon row of stalls, each one a little different from its neighbour in design and wares. The scene is more like the Middle East than staid old Ontario. A small sample of the outdoor market includes sweat suits, pencil sets, dish cloths, hub caps, matchbox toys and baseball cards. This is a great place to bring kids, for where else can you give a kid a buck and actually expect to receive change. That's right, there are lots of good old-fashioned flea-market items for much less than a dollar, so step right up, folks!

Stouffville Sales Barn

Inside the sales barn the scene is slightly more restrained but no less fun. Hawkers sell water conservation equipment, apple cider, costume jewellery and clothes. The same bargain prices as outside apply, for example socks at $12 a dozen pair and writing pads for 40 cents. Permanent shops located along the perimeter of the barn festive items from an auto mechanic's wish list: tool boxes, batteries, carburetors, wrenches and dollies of every type. There's also a large shop which sells pet accessories. And if you're the kind who can't have enough gadgets in your workshop, head for the hardware corner with bargains on tools, fasteners and cable. A large farmers' market extends from the east side of the barn. What a delightful place for a chef, especially in late summer or early fall, when the local harvest is at its peak. The vivid colour combinations make this place a joy, with purple eggplant, white cauliflower, crimson tomatoes and canary-yellow peppers, not to mention plums, blueberries, eggs, honey, and the most delectable garlic this side of Sicily. There are also more flea-market stalls on this side of the barn, with antiques, fire extinguishers, coat hangers (and vintage furs to cover them). Don't miss Tommy's Incredible $1 Bargain Barn, with an odd assortment of party favours, hair bands and tape. Next door is the Country Market Outlet. A fine name, but which country, one wonders, looking over the offerings of Chinese slippers, Belgian carpets, English soap and American towels.

If you decide to eat at the Stouffville Sales Barn, there are a number of places to find deli foods, both inside and outside the building. You may want to call it quits at this point and head back to Stouffville for a quieter meal away from the action. Head for the Corner House restaurant at Main and Church streets. The Corner House seems perfectly designed as an antidote for an overdose of flea market. It is congenial and calm with lots of comfort food, like freshly made soup, pasta and quiche (try the smoked salmon and leek). At dinner there's beef tenderloin, seafood and calves' liver. Experienced visitors check out the dessert board before planning their strategy, preferring to dine on trifle, meringue baskets with fresh fruit, or plum almandine (closed Sunday and Monday at lunch).

If the Sales Barn convinced you that shopping can be an enjoyable experience, try a stroll along Main Street in Stouffville. The Snowbird of Stouffville sells gifts with a Canadian flavour, such as wildlife prints, cedar eggs, moccasins and carvings. The Basket Jubilee and the Village Porch are good spots to buy gifts; there are even country-look sleeping baskets for Fido. Dave's Baseball Cards offers vintage and contemporary sports cards, Louisville sluggers and collector scorecards. On a distinctly more refined note, New England Collectibles has extraordinarily beautiful furniture, from Jacques & Hay marble-topped vanities to inlaid mahogany games tables. Across the street, Sheraton Antiques also has furniture to ooh and aah over, with lots of early Canadiana.

You may want to check out the Stouffville Bakery for cherry tarts or checkerboard cookies to munch on while driving home—if there's space among the work socks, Allen keys, snowsuits and other bargains picked up at Ontario's greatest shopping experience, the Stouffville Sales Barn.

Stouffville Sales Barn
Saturday 8:30-4:00
Sunday 9:30-4:00
(416) 640-3813

45

JACKSON'S POINT
A Trip for All Seasons

Many resort areas advertise themselves as "four-seasons" attractions, with recreation facilities suitable for each of Ontario's glorious seasons. But few locations can actually make good on such a promise. Fortunately, the area around Jackson's Point on the south shore of Lake Simcoe does deliver, with a mix of swimming, ice-fishing, country scenery and historic inns that can be appreciated year-round.

Begin by enjoying the bright blue waters of Lake Simcoe at Sibbald Point Provincial Park, 90 kilometres north of Toronto. Take Highway 48 north and turn left just after Sutton on County Road 18. Because the lake has been a popular vacation spot for generations, most of Simcoe's shoreline is built up and the traveller is limited to occasional glimpses of the lake through cottage properties that line the shore. But at Sibbald, all may enjoy summer sun on, in and under the water. There's a long, narrow strip of sand for sunbathers. A boat launch area and the rental of canoes, sailboats, sailboards and motorboats provide for fun out on the waves. Away from the crowds at the water's edge are sports fields, picnic sites and hiking trails. Park naturalists run a program of nature walks and workshops in activities from crafts to fish frying.

Sibbald is so popular that the wise daytripper schedules a visit for off-season or during the week. There's lots to do when the beach empties and autumn temperatures bring vivid colours to the countryside. The park runs a regulated pheasant shoot. The blue and white of winter brings opportunities for cross-country skiing (trails are marked but not groomed), skating, snowshoeing, snowmobiling (on the park road) and winter camping.

Sibbald Point includes Eildon Hall, the Regency-style home of the Sibbald family from 1836 until 1951. Matriarch Susan Sibbald immigrated to wild-and-woolly York County at the ripe old age of 53, and it was at Eildon Hall that she established what was

to become the centre of social life for the region. The house contains a few family artifacts, such as a china cabinet built around an old sea chest, silver serving pieces and portraits.

Sibbald, who worked hard to bring refinement to the backwoods, established St. George's Church, located just north of the park entrance. Look in the cemetery for the graves of Stephen Leacock and Mazo de la Roche.

After visiting St. George's, head west along the lakeshore to the town of Jackson's Point. At the eastern edge of town is the Red Barn Theatre, a prime location for summertime celebrity-spotting. The Red Barn specializes in Canadian drama, comedy and music, with a full slate of entertainment during July and August. Enjoy a local legend at bargain prices.

The Briars Inn & Country Club is truly a four-season resort, offering golf, tennis, water sports, and skiing on 200 acres which were once owned by the Sibbald family. The Briars has built a reputation for fine food and accommodation, friendly staff and a great children's program. It's a good spot for lunch for today's daytripper. Another option is the Georgina Inn, located right on the shoreline in Jackson's Point. This modern facility also offers a score of different sporting opportunities, from summer scuba diving to winter ice-skating on the frozen lake. For those who prefer to dine out of doors, picnic supplies abound at Alf's Deli in nearby Sutton: Black Forest ham, glorious seven-grain bread and brambleberry pie.

Jackson's Point caters to the needs of cottagers and travellers. No vacation town would be complete without ice-cream stands, and Jackson's Point has the Maple Leaf Dairy Bar and Vantage Point Ice Cream. Both sell ice cream in dozens of flavours, as well as other cool concoctions. Nostalgia sells old-time candies such as sponge toffee and butter balls. Other worthwhile visits include Tiffany Skye (clothing and antiques), Inanna (clothing),

The Briar's

Apples of Gold (country gifts and reproduction furniture), Country Heather (country collectibles), Books in the Attic (good travel and history section) and Crystal & Chimes (agate and amethyst gifts).

Jackson's Point caters to the sporting crowd. Lake Simcoe is renowned for angling—pike, pickerel, bass, perch, lake trout, whitefish. Bonnie Boats in Jackson's Point supplies boats and bait to the summer fisherman, and heated huts, tackle, food and lake transportation to the ice-fisherman. All you need is good luck.

Continue west along Lakeshore Road. If it's time to hit the beach again, there's Franklin Beach and Willow Beach just west of Jackson's Point. Both can get pretty congested on summer weekends, so stick to Sibbald or visit during the week. Sedate Roches Point is located where County Road 78 curves south around Cook's Bay. Many historic homes are located here, but unfortunately for the day-tripper, most are hidden by trees; visit in fall or winter for better viewing.

The daytrip to lake country ends at Keswick, where there are several more marinas that rent boating and fishing equipment. Try

Keffer Fish Hut Rentals, which not only rents equipment, but also provides an on-ice snack service for clients. Mercury Lodge also caters to ice-fishermen. For summer visitors, Keffer's and Miller's Marina (both on Lake Road) rent boats and motors, and supply tackle and other provisions.

You may have to wave goodbye to Ontario's four-season resort area for today, but it's comforting to know that whatever your outdoor pleasure, the southern shore of Lake Simcoe is a short drive away.

Sibbald Point Provincial Park
Daily 8:00 am-10:00 pm
Camping May-Thanksgiving and
December to mid-March
(416) 722-8061

The Briar's
(416) 722-3271

The Georgina Inn
(416) 722-6557

Red Barn Theatre
(416) 722-3249

46

UXBRIDGE
Looks are Deceiving

At first glance the hilly countryside of Uxbridge Township northeast of Toronto seems typical of southern Ontario: a quiet and prosperous landscape of regularly spaced farms surrounding an unassuming village. But the clever daytripper explores the ordinary in order to discover the extraordinary and finds that Uxbridge is home to several sites unique to Ontario. A day in the country blends a tour of these special places with uncrowded sideroad drives and relaxed small-town shopping.

The Uxbridge-Scott Museum provides a good orientation to the area. To reach the museum, drive west of Uxbridge along County Road 8 about 2 kilometres and turn north on Concession 6; the museum is a stone's throw along this road.

The museum chronicles the careers of several local residents. Displays provide information on Lucy Maud Montgomery, who resided in nearby Leaskdale from 1911 to 1926; pianist Glenn Gould, whose parents lived in Uxbridge; Group of Seven artist David Milne, who painted here during the 1940s; and Thomas Foster, whose memorial is one of Ontario's most unusual sights. An impressive collection of notables from one rural township.

The museum grounds include a collection of pioneer agricultural implements, the 9th Line United Church (used for modern-day weddings), and an Orange Lodge (the antique organs and pianos inside are relics from when Uxbridge was a major instrument-manufacturing town).

Drive into the town of Uxbridge by taking County Road 8 eastward. If it is time for lunch, consider a visit to the Hobby Horse Arms at 37 Main Street North (it has been serving commercial travellers since 1860). The downstairs pub is a pleasant place for lunch, serving workaday fare such as Welsh rarebit, ploughman's lunch and penny farthing salad. Upstairs, the dining room serves the landed gentry beef tenderloin, rabbit and salmon. The food and congenial service deserve rave reviews. Café 1806, on Brock Street downtown, serves a variety of fresh salads, sandwiches and pastas (closed Sunday). Next to the café is the Country Mercantile. Originally a bank, this shop has an interesting high tin ceiling and plays up its historic look with antiques, country decorating items and gifts. The public library is at Main and Brock. Not only is it a beautifully restored building, but the workings of the tower clock are encased in glass, on view inside the library.

Drive north on Main Street, which turns into County Road 1. No, your eyes aren't fooling you, that is a large dome sparkling through the trees a couple of kilometres north of town. The Thomas Foster Memorial may look like a limestone-and-copper Byzantine temple, but it was actually inspired by a visit to the Taj Mahal. No ordinary man, Foster (who spent his youth in Leaskdale) had a career as a butcher, mayor of Toronto and Member of Parliament. The memorial was a burial place for his wife Elizabeth and daughter Ruby. Foster, who died in 1945, is also buried here.

Public tours of the temple are conducted the first and third Sunday of every month from June until September (please call the museum to check dates and times). Don't miss an opportunity to tour this weird and wonderful landmark. The memorial is a marble palace decorated with ornate mosaics. It is the combination of colours that is most exceptional: marble in unusual black, green and plum, with mosaics and terrazzo flooring of delicate pinks and greens. The flooring design has visitors walking along the river Styx to the centre of the memorial, where eternal life radiates from Alpha and Omega. Real gold tiles glitter from the walls and domed ceiling. The Thomas Foster Memorial, built during Depression years for about $200,000, would represent a major undertaking for a large city, but it is nothing short of miraculous for tiny Uxbridge.

If you wish to do more Uxbridge touring, continue north on County Road 1 to Leaskdale.

Thomas Foster Memorial

A plaque on the lawn of an austere white house marks the home of Lucy Maud Montgomery. Scenes from *Road to Avonlea* were filmed in the vicinity, and museum staff are pleased to provide information on exact locations.

Southern Ontario's finest back-road driving is in the Uxbridge area. Head back through town to the 6th Concession (where the museum is located) and drive south. You'll pass an 1820 Quaker meeting house. Pennsylvania Quakers first settled the region in the early 1800s. There is something appealing about this unadorned board-and-batten building and its quiet setting. There is an annual service in June.

The 6th Concession south of town could be driven all day. Each hill crest reveals a view of farm and forest that is more perfect than the one before. The countryside is largely unspoiled by estate development and there are stretches where the narrow dirt roadway twists like a woodland trail, the trees an arm's length out the window. The scenery is beautiful year-round but is stunning during fall, with brilliant scarlet-and-orange maples and stately green pines.

Looks do deceive. You may have thought that Uxbridge was an ordinary farm town. But where else can you see Ontario's Taj Mahal, Lucy Maud Montgomery's home, a Quaker meeting house, and a 130-year-old inn all within a ten-minute drive? Ordinary Ontario? Extraordinary!

Uxbridge-Scott Museum
Mid-May to mid-October:
Wednesday-Sunday & Holidays
10:00-5:00
(416) 852-5854

Thomas Foster Memorial tours
June-September:
1st and 3rd Sundays
(phone to check on schedule)
(416) 852-6855

47

PICKERING
A Walk Through Time

Living in a highly urbanized environment makes it easy to lose touch with our past, to forget (or never to learn) how the land might have looked before subdivisions and highways, how our forebears might have worked and played before mass production and mass marketing. Spend a day in Pickering and take a walk back through time to when settlements were small and forest trees were tall.

A hint at the natural beauty of old Ontario can be had by walking Pickering's Seaton hiking trail, a project of the Ontario Ministry of Housing and the Metro Toronto and Region Conservation Authority. This well-used (but not overused) hiking trail follows the west branch of Duffin's Creek for about 10 kilometres, from Grand Valley Park in Pickering north to the hamlet of Green River at Highway 7. Although much of the area to the south has been used for urban development, the Ontario Land Corporation holds over 12,000 hectares in the area around Duffin's Creek, explaining why this particular valley remains in a natural state.

The trail comprises three sections, the middle or wilderness portion being the most recommended. (Contact the Ontario Land Corporation in Toronto for a detailed trail guide.) Exit the 401 at Port Union Road, drive east on Kingston Road to Altoona Road; drive north to the 3rd Concession and turn east; make a northward turn on White's Road (second road east of Altoona). Clarke's Hollow is where the road crosses Duffin's Creek. There is a signposted parking area. Follow the trail (it is signed and well-worn) on the south side of the river, heading west and north. It is about 3.8 kilometres to the village of Whitevale.

The trail climbs high above the river, with several beautiful views opening up through the trees (visitors are asked to be cautious near the unstable cliff edges). Fragrant cedar, hemlock and pine cover the slopes, some estimated to be 300 to 400 years old, meaning that they were here when Indians hunted and fished the valley. While there are some steep climbs and a couple of river crossings, the way has been made easier by stairways, log bridges and a rest area halfway along. The high ground has areas of abandoned farmland, which provides an excellent opportunity to study the regeneration of native forest. These areas between the woodland and pasture, known as "edge" habitat, attract deer and songbirds. The valley bottom lands are also a good place to study natural processes, as the openings left by dying elms are taken over by tangles of wild grape and cedar.

If you are a keen walker, continue along all the way to Whitevale. If not, return to the car and drive north on the Altoona Road to Whitevale Road and then east to town. There is a parking lot on the west side of the river, along with a playground and picnic area. To find the trail, cross the bridge and head north through the mill yard. This portion of the trail examines the relationship between the river and human activity. The grist mill at Whitevale is the only one that remains of the many which located along Duffin's Creek.

A short distance along the trail is the original dam site for the Whitevale Mill. It was built about a century ago and remained water-powered until 1975. The millrace gates are still visible, and the rush of water over the dam is still heard from quite a distance away. Whitevale is an attractive village and many of its board-and-batten homes are excellent examples of domestic architecture of the last century.

Country-fresh air and exercise will stir the appetite. The best idea might be to take a brown-bag lunch for the trail. Otherwise, enjoy lunch at the Peppercorn Mill at the corner of Altoona Road and Finch Avenue. The daily lunch buffet will fill up any hiker and the atmosphere is pleasant.

Pickering

After viewing the countryside as it might have looked in days of yore, head north to Highway 7 and then east to Greenwood and the Pickering Museum Village. The village comprises about 13 buildings in scenic parkland on the east branch of Duffin's Creek and presents life in the area from the mid-nineteenth century to early twentieth century. (If you've left lunch till this point, the picnic grounds here are very agreeable.)

Domestic life is described through exhibits in a primitive log cabin, the plank home of an established farm family, and a merchant's board-and-batten home; commercial structures include the Brougham Central Hotel, Duffin's Creek General Store, and a woodworking shop; there are also several barns and two churches. Most buildings are from the Pickering-Brougham-Greenwood area. The village jumps with activity on special-event days, with demonstrations of spinning, butter-making, baking, woodworking and smithing.

The claim to fame of the Pickering Museum Village is the remarkable collection of gasoline and steam engines, housed in their own complex. The collection emphasizes farm equipment such as tractors and threshers, and industrial machinery from sawmills. The museum also has an assortment of wagons, sleighs and cutters.

A visit to Pickering leaves us more aware of what Ontario was like before the days of theme parks and shopping malls.

Pickering Museum Village
June & September:
Saturday, Sunday & Holidays 11:00-5:00
July & August:
Wednesday-Sunday 11:00-5:00
(416) 683-8401

48

WHITBY
The Grass is Always Greener...

On the Cullens' side of the fence. Or ... so you may conclude after spending a day at Cullen Gardens in Whitby. Cullen Gardens offers four seasons of outdoor and indoor activities so varied that even the purple thumb will find something of value. Make your way to one of the prettiest spots in southern Ontario by driving east on the 401, north about 6 kilometres on Highway 12 and west on Taunton Road. The gardens are just west of the intersection of Highway 12 and Taunton.

Where to start a Cullen tour? Head for the miniature village, where over 250 buildings at 1/12 scale are displayed in a setting of dwarf shrubs, flower beds and hand-clipped grass. You won't find a hokey Eiffel Tower here, but finely crafted replicas of historic homes, churches and businesses, many from the Durham area. The village is not a static display and children especially enjoy spotting all the animated characters (bet ya can't find all 600!). Firefighters douse a house fire, a farmer chops wood in the barnyard, and a child extracts a kite from a tree. Cottage Country includes models of some of Muskoka's most famous resorts and holiday spots, with provincial camp grounds, marinas and ferries, cars and trains.

Of course, Cullen Gardens is also acres of gardens. In the topiary area, trees and shrubs are clipped into the shapes of various creatures. Enormous living sculptures are formed by filling an iron skeleton with soil and then planting thousands of begonia, telanthera and santolina. Islands of roses and other flowers are meticulously cared for, and the plants express their appreciation by providing abundant colour and perfume over a long growing season. Gardeners will be interested to know that Cullen Gardens has a display of the prestigious All America selections of annuals—plants judged to be superior specimens in many categories. The seed from the All America garden is usually available the year after display. Another miniature area can be found in the valley, this one a model of a

country fair, complete with rides and midway hawkers. Last but not least there is the amphitheatre, where plays for adults and puppet shows for kids run from May to October; during inclement weather, the performances are held in the Tea Room.

The Cullen Garden staff run a busy schedule of events throughout the year. Late April marks the beginning of spring, with over 100,000 bulbs offering brilliant relief for eyes weary of winter greys. Migrating trout and salmon can be spotted in the garden stream and the shops take on a Dutch theme. June and July mark the Rose Festival, with over 2,000 bushes at the peak of their bloom, while after dark there are fireworks over the pond. September is the time to visit for chrysanthemums ranging from apricot to deepest orange. Perhaps the most beautiful time of year at Cullen Gardens is during the Festival of Lights (mid-November to early January), when the area is transformed into a sparkly wonderland with millions of lights, a nativity scene, carollers, hot chocolate and a Christmas show. A winter carnival in January is replete with sled dogs, ice sculptures and bonfires.

If you think the action is all out of doors, you're in for a big surprise. Indoors, there might be a pumpkin-carving contest or a performance by an international choir. Shoppers will be glad to find offerings of women's and men's apparel, crafts and gifts (from china collectibles to books), and Cullen Gardens souvenirs. Snacks and light meals are available in the Solarium Café. Don't let the elegant decor of the Garden Gate Restaurant stop you from enjoying a good meal. Although beautiful and quiet, the restaurant is kid-friendly and the huge windows allow a terrific view of Cottage Country. The Garden Gate serves sandwiches, pasta and quiche among its lunch dishes, and roasts and seafood at dinner.

A fairly recent addition to Cullen Gardens is the 1812 Lynde House, accurately billed as a

Cullen Gardens

"museum with a difference." Jabez Lynde was the local pathmaster and sheriff, as well as a farmer; his home was relocated from Highway 2 and restored. Rather than the conventional museum tour, animated figures are used to portray family life during the nineteenth century—an interesting combination of Disney and *Little House on the Prairie.* Children pop out of closets in a game of hide-and-seek, a baby is comforted, and laundry is washed. The basement of Lynde House has a display of historic photographs of Whitby and surrounding villages.

Opposite the entrance to Cullen Gardens is a gravel laneway leading to a Weall & Cullen garden centre. If the magical combination of landscape architecture and horticulture at the gardens left you with ideas for the home scene, you'll find everything you need to get started, from plants to design guides, as well as items for the interior decorator.

The Cullen Gardens people have done something truly miraculous in proving that, despite the inhospitable climate, Canadian gardens can be enjoyed daily year-round. Come to Whitby and see for yourself.

Cullen Gardens
Garden Gate Restaurant
Daily 11:00-10:00

Grounds & Shops
Mid-April to mid-January:
Daily, extended hours during
summer and Christmas season
(416) 668-6606
(416) 294-7965

49

OSHAWA
Living Legend

The stereotypical Canadian hero, so Hollywood tells us, is the strong and silent type—a backwoodsman, a flying ace, a Mountie—a loner quietly doing a noble deed and then slipping unnoticed into historical obscurity. Spend a day in Oshawa living with Colonel R.S. McLaughlin, whose life as an industrial tycoon and philanthropist exemplifies a wholly different genre of Canadian hero.

Robert Samuel McLaughlin was born in 1871. His father was a Scots immigrant farmer and carriage-maker. Robert became Canada's most important early industrialist when he convinced his father to begin the manufacture of "horseless carriages" in 1908. Thus, Oshawa was set on the path to becoming the automotive capital of Canada. The McLaughlin company became part of the General Motors empire, with R.S. McLaughlin president of the Canadian branch and vice-president of the North American corporation. The best place to begin our hero's story is the Canadian Automotive Musuem at 99 Simcoe Street in Oshawa. Exit the 401 at Simcoe Street and drive north, following signs to the museum.

If you think that auto showrooms are not for you, it's time to think again. This museum is full of Canadian history, technological wonders and gleaming beauty. The collection of 80 vintage autos dates back to the 1898 Fisher Electric and includes the McLaughlin touring cars of 1908 and 1912. McLaughlin struck a deal with Will Durant (founder of General Motors) to build Buicks with McLaughlin bodies, hence the 1922 McLaughlin Buick. This car had a racing version, a record holder at 87.5 miles per hour (set in 1911).

There's a 1915 Ford Model "T" built in Windsor, and Stratford's 1925 Brooks Steamer, which ran on steam power. Find out about the other early Canadian auto towns, such as Galt (the 1914 Galt Electric car, the first with turn signals), Chatham (the 1921 Gray Dort), Kitchener

Parkwood

(the 1903 Redpath Messenger), Orillia (the 1908 Tudhope McIntyre) and Brockville (the beautiful 1914 Atlas Model "G"). Modern pieces of interest include the 1965 Amphicar from West Germany, capable of travelling by land or sea, and the infamous 1975 Bricklin.

Business success led to great wealth for McLaughlin, represented in part by his 55-room Greek Revival mansion known as Parkwood. Drive north on Simcoe to the intersection with Adelaide; the tall green fence marks the Parkwood estate. Begin a visit by taking the informative and thorough house tour.

Designed by Darling & Pearson (also responsible for the Canadian Parliament Buildings) and built in 1917, Parkwood must have been one of the country's most luxurious homes. The grand entry is impressive, with its cantilevered curved staircase, lavish murals and organ pipes hidden behind silk damask panels. The oak-panelled drawing room follows suit—rich in tapestry, white marble, glittering chandeliers and a Steinway concert piano. Parkwood is a study in furniture design, with rooms in Louis XIV, Chippendale, Queen Anne and Art Deco; all have remarkable woodwork, and imported carpets and antiques, left just as the family had them. Upper rooms contain a collection of art works from the Group of Seven and from McLaughlin's daughter Isabel, an accomplished painter.

Parkwood portrays McLaughlin as more than just a fabulously wealthy man. He was also a family man, and despite its grandeur the home exudes a warm and congenial atmosphere (like the reading lamps cleverly recessed into the twin beds in the master bedroom, and the favourite armchair in the garden room). McLaughlin was a considerate employer: he had additions made to his home and gardens to provide employment for auto workers laid off during the 1930s depression.

McLaughlin was a sportsman and his home includes a bowling alley, squash court and pool, while the billiard room contains many yachting trophies. McLaughlin was also a lover of ideas and learning, attested to by the library of 1,000 volumes. There are many special items here, like the original 1911 Encyclopedia Britannica with onionskin pages and suede jacket. Family life, good works, intellect—sound like a recipe for success? Must

be, for McLaughlin lived at Parkwood until his death in his 101st year.

Parkwood is more than a house. Summer visitors also tour the fabulous gardens, which are as lavish and varied as the house. There's an Italian water garden, Japanese garden, formal garden, and a large greenhouse attached to the home. The garden teahouse serves light meals during the summer months. It's the best place to eat on today's tour.

Philanthropist McLaughlin donated a library and hospital wing to Oshawa, buildings to York University and the University of Guelph, and the McLaughlin Planetarium to Toronto. The family generosity lives on in other ways. The McLaughlin Art Gallery was donated to Oshawa by Ewart McLaughlin, grandson of Robert McLaughlin Sr. (Robert Samuel's father), who was an amateur painter. This first-rate gallery features changing exhibits with an emphasis on Canadian works, especially those of the Painters 11.

You might expect to visit Oshawa to envy the wealth of Sam McLaughlin, but you will come away with admiration for his business acumen, personal integrity and public largesse. A Canadian hero writ large.

Canadian Automotive Museum
Monday-Friday 9:00-5:00
Saturday & Sunday 10:00-6:00
(416) 576-1222

Parkwood
house, gardens and tea house
June-August:
Tuesday-Sunday 10:30-4:30
house only
April, May, September to
mid-December:
Tuesday-Friday and Sunday 1:30-4:30
also, garden open for November
chrysanthemum show
(416) 579-1311

Robert McLaughlin Gallery
Tuesday & Thursday 10:00-9:00
Wednesday & Friday 10:00-6:00
Saturday & Sunday 12:00-5:00
(416) 576-3000

50

PORT PERRY
Scoot to Scugog

Picture this: a pretty, historic downtown; bright blue waters reflecting scores of boats; a local history museum; all this surrounded by farm markets and provided with a most friendly welcome. Too good to be true? Fortunately not, for Port Perry is alive and well and waiting to be visited. The Port is easy to find; just drive north from the 401 on Highway 7/12.

Queen Street, Port Perry's main drag, is simply one of the most engaging streets you'll find anywhere. Dichromatic brick, multi-paned windows, lace curtains, reproduction lamps and hanging baskets will have you thinking you've stepped into the nineteenth century. And best of all, Port Perry has not yet made it into the tourism big leagues, meaning that there are kilometres of uncrowded sidewalks and plenty of parking places.

The shopping is terrific. The Creative Basket is worth seeing just for the exquisite antique storefront and interior appointments; this is the spot for British and Canadian gourmet food items. Nuts About Chocolate is another store that plays up the historic, with a 1926 candy dispenser and goodies you haven't seen since childhood. Gumballs, jelly bellies and misty mints are side by side with Belgian chocolates filled with black currant, cherry swirl or Irish cream. History never tasted so good.

Cross the street to a bevy of stores centred on postcard-perfect Settlement House. The Settlement House, Linen Corner, Luke's Country Store and Daisy's Fabrics carry everything you'll need for that fashionable country interior: linens and draperies, cotton rugs and scented candles, wreaths and brass collectibles. Port Perry even has a friendly welcome for young shoppers: the Children's Den and Ted E. Bears sell clothing and toys. Art collectors will want to check out Port Gifts on Queen Street and Kay's Place on Water Street for names such as Lumbers, Bateman or Parker. Around the Corner is

well named; turn off Queen onto Perry Street to find the building, which houses the Cottage Rose, the Bear Shoppe and the Wheat Sheaf Café.

The delights of Port Perry extend to lunch. The best place to find out what's happening in town is Hank's Bakery; regulars meet here for a morning coffee that lasts past noon. Cornish pasties, sausage rolls, cookies, and sweet and savory breads—the prices will have you wondering if Port Perry is stuck in the nineteenth century. Locals point with pride to Murray House, which features fine dining in a restored old home (no lunch on weekends, closed Monday). Every port has a chippery, and Port Perry's Galley Fish and Chips uses an English-style batter on their fish. Emiel's reflects the cultural heritage of the region, with part of the menu printed in Dutch; large portions for the meat-and-potatoes crowd and more small-town chatter.

An après-lunch ramble along the waterfront should be next on your agenda. What a thoroughly pleasant place to be on a summer's day: kids in the playground, music in the band shell, sunlight dancing on the water. The marina rents boats and canoes. Lake Scugog is at the frontier of southern Ontario, where farmland and cottage country meet and commingle, making the lake an interesting tour in itself.

Drive south on Water Street to Scugog Street (Highway 7A) and turn east. Slow down to admire the fine marsh along the causeway. There are feeding herons here during summer and masses of migrating birds during spring and fall. If you've brought your rod and reel, join your peers along the shoreline.

Follow signs just east of town for the short drive to the Scugog Shores Museum. This modest local museum is located in a country schoolhouse and features artifacts collected from the local area. The mock-ups include a trading post (a realistic jumble of fabric, coffee beans and candy jars), a post office and a

Settlement House, Port Perry

pharmacy. The area's best-known resident, cartoonist James Llywellyn Rise, was born near here. His renderings of Birdseye Centre, capturing the humorous interaction of city dwellers and country folk, endeared him to newspaper readers early in this century. Some of his cartoons are displayed. The museum is a good vantage point for viewing the bucolic countryside and savouring the fragrance of newly cut hay.

An afternoon can be spent visiting local farm markets (Port Perry has its own at the fair-grounds) and country fairs (Port Perry's is on Labour Day weekend). Or visit roadside stands and sample strawberries, honey or apples.

When big-city life has you hankering for some place to slow down, treat yourself to a Port Perry dose of congenial hospitality, engaging architecture and pleasant scenery.

Scugog Shores Museum
May-October:
Daily 1:00-5:00
(416) 985-3589

BIBLIOGRAPHY

Information on tourist attractions came from a multitude of sources. Government publications and brochures printed by public and private facilities are too numerous to mention, but the following published sources deserve recognition.

Brown, Ron. *Backroads of Ontario.* Edmonton: Hurtig, 1984.

Dahms, Fredric A. *The Heart of the Country.* Deneau: Toronto, 1988.

Filey, Mike. *A Walker's, Jogger's, Cycler's, Boater's Guide to Toronto's Waterfront.* Toronto of Old: Toronto, 1989.

Gould, Allan. *The Toronto Book.* Key Porter: Toronto, 1983.

Gregory, Dan, and Roderick MacKenzie. *Toronto's Backyard: A Guide to Selected Nature Walks.* Douglas & McIntyre: Vancouver, 1986.

Hardy, Anne, editor. *Where to Eat in Canada.* Ottawa: Oberon, 1988.

Horner, Gary. *The Bicycle Guide to Southwestern Ontario.* Lone Pine: Edmonton, 1989.

Issenman, JoAnn. *The Adventurous Torontonian's Food Guide.* Tundra: Montreal, 1989.

McHugh, Patricia. *Toronto Architecture: A City Guide.* McClelland & Stewart: Toronto, 1985.

McInnes, Craig. "Renowned Fish Returning to Ontario River." *The Globe and Mail* (Toronto), October 20, 1990, p.A6.

Reznik, Allan. *Ontario Cross-Country Skiing Guide.* Fenn: Mississauga, 1985.

Ruprecht, Tony. *Toronto's Many Faces.* Whitecap: Toronto, 1990.

Sewell, John and Charlotte Sykes. *Rowland Travel Guide to Toronto.* Series edited by Wade Rowland. Rowland & Jacob: Toronto, 1988.

Snowden, Annette. *Discover Southern Ontario.* Toronto: Irwin, 1985.

Stoddart Publishing. *1990 Stoddart Restaurant Guide to Toronto.* General Paperbacks: Toronto, 1990.

Weiler, Merike, and Dini Petty. *Kid-Bits.* Methuen: Toronto, 1987.

THE BOSTON MILLS PRESS